Steve!

Thanks for inspiring me to Get Seen.

Thanks also for being a Friend since the Golden Age of Podcasting,

John

B2B Marketing Confessions

B2B Marketing Confessions

John J. Wall

ISBN 978-1-300021-018

Table of Contents

Acknowledgments

This book is dedicated to Beverly Marcus Wall. Thank you for giving me your love of reading.

First and foremost I thank the lovely Carin for putting up with everything that goes along with putting up with me, including the delusion that most of the time I've got a 50/50 shot at success. Dad, Mom and Jason, thanks for being around when all of this started with a TRS-80 computer, and then me selling off the parts years later.

Thanks to Judith Miller who taught a young man how to write, and Carol Meinhart who taught a young businessman how to market.

To the Podcamp duo of Christopher S. Penn, who enriches and refines my marketing skills weekly, and Chris Brogan, who not only inspired me to write this but told me directly to do it over dessert wine, thanks, this would not have happened without you.

I've had the privilege of working with a number of authors as part of podcasting and *Marketing Over Coffee* (MoC). It's been great to have front row seats for the David Meerman Scott show, thanks for seeking me out to learn more about podcasting all those years ago. The greatest unexpected benefit of MoC was getting to talk with Simon Sinek, who inspires me every business day. I always said that I would consider MoC a success if I had a chance to interview Seth Godin, thanks to him for making that come true.

I cannot say enough about the friends I've met over the past 8 years. For the first half of my career I worked alone, many of my managers understood my results but had no idea what I was doing or how I did it. With the explosion of blogging and podcasting I was blessed with new peers and friends, people like Ron Ploof that I compare notes with every week. Other friends from the golden age of podcasting: Mitch Joel, Joseph Jaffe, Julien Smith, C.C. Chapman, Franklin McMahon, Bob Knorpp, Steve Garfield, John Blue, Tim Street, and Eric Schwartzman (I'm sure I'm missing a few here).

The Amazing Ed Healy introduced me to Troy Taylor who edited an early draft of this book, and cleaned up all the run-on sentences in this book, or at least most of them, I wrote this intro after he was done working on the book. Author Jason M. Wall introduced me to Meridith Merchant, and both of them gave significant feedback on the readability of this book. If any errors, factual or editorial, still exist in this book I'm going to blame them. I'm sure there are people who have inspired me that I've missed, being unable to easily blame anyone for those, I'll apologize now and take blame for that myself.

"Look out for each other and never give up" – J.T.K.

Introduction

"The beginning is the most important part of the work."
-Plato

T his book has been on my mind for about five years. I've been fortunate enough to work at a number of companies in which the marketing function was built from zero to upwards of $40 million dollars. When I began, the phenomenon of personal computers was just beginning to scratch the surface of the business world. I had a front-row seat to watch email become the cornerstone of business communications, see customer records go from a ratty paper folder on some sales guy's desk to a digital nervous system that lives up in the cloud, and marketing transform from TV advertising and PR agencies to its own technological industry.

I have waited to write this book because I knew if I fell into the tired model of "throw out three or four big concepts and mix in case studies to taste" that it would be boring to write and boring to read. I've read hundreds of business books over the past decade and noticed that if you look at many publications four years later you see many of the celebrated companies out of business. Worse yet, there is the handful of companies that are so successful that they can be used to "prove" pretty much anything. The reality is that just because a tactic worked for someone else, it doesn't necessarily mean it will do anything for you. Rather than tell the story of Apple or Zappos for the millionth time, I wanted to talk about as many different tactics as I could cover and what I've learned from trying them.

Over the years I gathered notes on the tactics that truly work. As the "Procedures" folder grew and grew, I soon had a utility belt that I could take with me anywhere and share with anyone who had questions. Often this would fuel my blog, and then later the *Marketing Over Coffee* podcast.

Four Key Points

For the purpose of this book marketing is organized around four key points:

1. Designing a Great Product: The Product Marketing Function
2. Telling the World: Marketing Demand Generation
3. Education: The Sales Function
4. Customer Retention: Serve to Keep Customers Happy

You may already know where you are weak and strong on these points. If not, you will once you've explored what is offered in this book and have seen some results.

We also cover the strategic issues to think about with your Customer Relationship Management (CRM) System, and those that involve social media technologies.

Many tactics are discussed from the ground up, so you have more to work with than just the 50,000-foot view.

Feel free to jump around if there are sections that are more appropriate for your situation. Unless you are brand new to marketing a product, odds are that you're already using a number of these tactics. There are some tactics that cover more than one point. I have addressed them under the key point that they most commonly reside. For example, email is addressed in Telling the World: Marketing Demand Generation.

Basic Salesforce.com Concepts

Being effective requires access to accurate information. You need the equivalent of a computer genius sidekick working from a hidden base or your own supercomputer in the cave underneath your stately manor. Before I begin, please note that throughout the book I will use CRM and Salesforce.com interchangeably.

I've found Salesforce.com to be a superb solution that is constantly improving and consider it the gold standard. If you are using some other CRM system you probably have similar functionality for most of the basic tactics. If you are not familiar with the basic structure of Salesforce.com, the rest of this section will bring you up to speed. (If you *are* familiar with leads, contacts, accounts, opportunities and how these objects relate to each other, then feel free to jump ahead.)

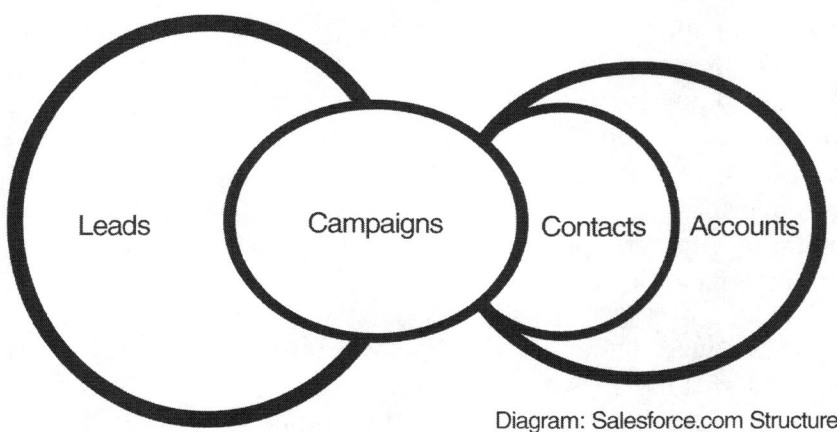

Diagram: Salesforce.com Structure

There are 4 objects (tables of data) that are at the core of the system. *Leads* are people that could possibly be customers. These are the people that you will be trying to make aware of your product. Some of your leads may have been engaged by your sales force, and eventually, if the salesperson believes that there is a possibility of selling them something, two things take place. First, if a lead is "real" it is converted to a *Contact*. As far as the data, a contact has the same basic layout as a lead: phone, email, mailing address, and a list of previous activities. But there's one key difference—every contact is associated with an *Account*. For example, if Bob works for Acme Corp and he is converted to a contact, he will be connected to a record for Acme Corp (Acme's Account record). The benefit here is that as your relationship with numerous employees at a single organization grows, you can look at the Account record, which will roll up all of the previous activities of all the Contacts at the Account.

Whereas a *Lead* is often missing key information and will usually have no relationship built with your organization, when the key information is obtained, the *Contact* is created so you can see the relationship between the individual and the organization, and you can manage the *Account* as a whole.

When a lead is converted to a contact the contact owner also is presented with the option to create an opportunity. An opportunity is a record that has the information on a possible sale (information along the lines of "This contact is looking at product X for $Y and will buy in the next month"). It's very common for a lead to convert to a contact and an opportunity to be created at the same time. The opportunity can have additional contacts attached to it and opportunity records are what fuel the sales forecast. By looking at all open opportunities, management has as close to an accurate forecast as it is going to get.

I'll explain more later. Specifically, we'll look at how this process can be used to manage the effectiveness of your marketing programs. The number of lead conversions and opportunities created and closed are data points that tell you what kind of bang you are getting for your buck.

A disclaimer—the majority of organizations I have worked with had fewer than 150 employees. I have noticed that the concept of Dunbar's number does seem to hold—regardless of the size of your organization there really aren't many effective teams with over 150 people. In theory, the success of smaller groups should scale to larger teams but politics and bureaucracy grows as teams expand beyond the size of an average person knowing everyone on a first name basis. Larger organizations tend to have far more complex political structures. Regardless of the fact that the small group around you will probably behave like any other organization of its size, there's always the possibility that something you do will affect something way up or down the chain and cause trouble, or huge success, somewhere that you did not intend or suspect. Nobody wants that surprise visit from the home office.

On the other hand, in a larger organization, you are less likely to have the small business "build everything from duct tape and chicken wire" syndrome that can make the exceptional marketing concept look more like a shanty town for the homeless.

As we explain the four points, we outline tactics. No matter how much you read there is no substitute for trying these tactics. It may be difficult just to get permission to try something new, and it will test your ability to sell new concepts—an invaluable skill in getting yourself out of the cube farm and into a position at a better pay grade.

Your Own Progression

There are a few things to keep in mind as you apply tactics for the first time and as you become a more skilled marketer.

As you start, you have no experience. Everything you do is an opportunity to learn. At no point in your journey will you be as bombarded with new experiences, and this is where you will experience your most spectacular failures. The good news is that even the second try will be significantly easier than the first. The good news is that if you are in a new market or technology, if you are the first person to take the beatings, the market tends to reward you disproportionally (the first technology startups tend to make a lot more cash than the fifth startup on the scene, which usually goes nowhere). My goal in writing this his book is to help you understand just what the hell is going on, and to tech you how to avoid the worst beatings so you will succeed.

Once you have a rough idea of what you're doing, you will have realized most of the value of these tactics. As you get more comfortable you'll begin to tackle larger challenges. If you've been getting your company into "social media" and you have an active blog driving traffic that leads to your website, you are getting most of the value you can out of your programs. Though you could continue messing around with technologies that showed up on the scene a few hours ago and enhance what you are doing, odds are, they are not going to deliver enough to be worthwhile. When your marketing tactics reach this stage, fine tune to make the process as efficient as possible—automate as much as you can so that it becomes as cost effective as you can make it. These projects often become "boring" and just sit there unattended making money. The list of people I know who don't worry about money because they are doing "boring" stuff is absurdly long. Once your process is fine tuned, schedule it for a checkup in a few quarters or next year and experiment with something new.

Ultimately my hope is that you go beyond this book to create and use your own tactics. There is great value in being the best in the world at the tactic you specialize in. This is how agencies deliver value that their clients are not able to attain. The bad news is that marketing has become so integrated with technology that this skill level continually climbs higher and higher. Tactics and strategies only available to the elite eventually become simple enough that anyone can apply them and as a marketer you are forced into a constant state of creating the "next big thing."

Regardless of your skill level in any tactic, this book was created to help you get more done in less time. I can't guarantee success for you, but at least you don't have to learn the hard way about some of the obstacles that I've hit at 200 miles per hour. The good news is that tactics that crash and burn will do you no physical harm.

Best of luck with your adventures,
John
john@themshow.com
www.B2BMarketingConfessions.com

Key Point #1

Designing a Great Product: The Product Marketing Function

Strategy: Great Design

"A designer knows he has achieved perfection not when there is nothing more to add, but when there is nothing left to take away."
- Antoine de Saint-Exupéry

I've never met anyone who had a huge idea, started to run with it, created a business that was acquired or sold, and rode off into the sunset. The successful people I know started with their best shot and then adjusted and pivoted as they slowly learned what people are *actually willing to pay for.*

This chapter is rather short. That's because, ultimately, design is art. There are great books out there, such as *The Design of Everyday Things* by Donald A. Norman, which explain the principles and techniques. But there is no substitute for experience. You can read all the books you want on painting or water skiing, but there is no substitute for picking up a brush or jetting behind a boat. Any books you read will become much more useful after you've made a few attempts and have a feel for what it's really like.

We are talking about business, so that focuses our discussion of design. The end goal of our labor is to provide value to our customer, which in turn, means you get paid. You will design, see how the market responds, redesign, and repeat.

Of course, this means that there will be many failures, and much has already been written about how our culture has beaten the fear of failure into us so well, that it is ingrained in the behavior of the majority. Fear of standing out and being different is so rampant that those who take the chances, the entrepreneurs, mavericks, and artists—have the opportunity for huge financial gain over those who "work for the man."

I will refer to Simon Sinek's *Start With Why* many times. If you are not aware of Simon and his work, at the very least, take 18 minutes to watch his 2009 TedX presentation (http://www.youtube.com/watch?v=u4ZoJKF_VuA). Defining **why** you are taking action focuses your design. Between understanding why you are taking action and your desire to please your customers enough for them to part with their hard-earned cash, you now have the guardrails visible as you begin your voyage. There is another benefit to starting with "Why": it allows your business to scale rapidly. When you have defined your purpose in simple terms, it's easy for everyone in the organization to understand what needs to be done.

Sinek uses the Celery Test to illustrate "Why" and "Scale" in action. All the options you have in designing a product or service can be compared to a trip through the grocery store—you may try this or that and have things in the cart that you've used before. If you don't have a clear statement of "Why," you are aimlessly wandering through the grocery store. If you layer on top of that a clear statement of "Why" such as: "To eat healthy foods" suddenly it's much clearer what should be in the cart—yes to the fruits and vegetables (like celery!) and no to soft drinks and no to Sugar Bombs, the only sweetened cereal dipped in chocolate.

In my quest to improve my marketing skills, I have read many books on product marketing and have waded through thousands of pages. It all boils down to two messages:

1. Simplicity is Beautiful Design.
2. Preference (An Expression of Personality) Changes Over Time.

These two factors explain why, even after more than a century of building cars, you still need to have a warranty. You'd think that by now, someone would build a car that required no maintenance in the first 5 years, but the target is always in motion. Consumers want bigger vehicles, ones that use less fuel, or ones that don't look like those their parents drove. Manufacturers make vehicles that look "cooler" than their competitors, appealing to human emotion, rather than performance.

Simplicity is Beautiful Design

Sir William Hamilton first wrote of Occam's Razor—a philosophical argument that the simplest theories ought to be used unless you can trade simplicity for more powerful functionality. Please note that this is a simplification of the argument, you will find Occam's Razor debated endlessly in many places. Ironically, people cannot agree on a way to express a principle of simplicity in a simple way.

This "no extra stuff" school of design (showcased by Apple) is classic. Rarely is a design condemned for rounded corners and smooth finishes. If you are making a device that plays music, or hosting a guest at your hotel, if everything takes as few steps as possible, and never has any harsh or rough contact, odds are you'll do well. Or at least better than the guy down the street with the product that's more difficult to work, or makes the customer feel stupid or angry.

There are only two ways to do this:

1. A genius will foresee all needs and outcomes and get it right the first time.
2. The other 99.9% will take an iterative process—Try. Adjust. Try again.

So, get working.

Preference Changes Over Time

As an economist, I often fantasize over what the world would be like if simplicity reigned (yes, economists tend to be oddballs). My previously mentioned maintenance-free cars would need service only for accidents or after 200,000 miles when they've taken a beating from the weather. I'd never stare at unmarked knobs in a hotel shower stall puzzling over which one is the hot water. I wouldn't have spent a measurable portion of my life setting up my family's VCRs to record shows, (and fixing the flashing 12:00 on the clock). Alas, this is folly. We are human and we get tired of things, few have the perseverance to design all the way to perfection.

On one side are the customers. For better or worse, they will judge the things they buy and so will everyone around them. They may care about the statements their possessions make, or they may not. Their neighbors may judge them, or not care. Nonetheless, when a 1972 station wagon rattles down a street belching smoke, it's generating an emotional response:

Owner:	"This car has served me well."
Green neighbor:	"That thing is causing more cancer than second-hand smoke."
Nostalgic friend:	"It's a classic woody!"
Worried parent:	"Johnson should have his license taken away. He's a threat."

Every product bought or sold has an emotional impact on both sides and the rest of the world at large. Intended or inadvertent emotional impact causes designs to be changed and experimented with. The fashion and jewelry industries exist only because purchases have an emotional, as well as functional, impact on our lives.

Does a $12,000 watch have functionality that your average $40 watch does not? Yes, it will impress some people; others will feel important wearing it. Again—that's why this is an art—not a hard science. How people feel about what they buy is as important to design as the parts that hold it together.

Another factor is that the designer is not without ego. The person promoted to create the next iteration of a line of vehicles may not be as interested in fine-tuning all of the features and functions of previous versions as pushing a new look or adding completely new features to the product. Or worse yet from a predictability standpoint, this same person may opt to "start from scratch" and build it "from the ground up." As a result, those who value predictability in maintenance will avoid the first model year; those thirsting for something new will flock to it. The media, getting paid to cover the novel and interesting, will run pictures of the new model. Who wants to read an article about how the 15th version of the existing model eked out an additional mile per gallon?

Strategy: Three Steps to Designing Great Things

"Well begun is half done."
-Aristotle

An entire school of marketing called Product Marketing has developed from activities that determine what a product should be, who will buy it, and how it should be sold. In many companies, there is a visionary who takes on this role. In larger organizations there is one person that takes the input from one or more visionaries and then mixes it in with feedback from either internal testers or possible/existing customers. This is a critical position. Actions taken here will set the course of the product and often determine if it will live or die, long before it hits the shelves (even if the shelves are virtual).

Over the past 10 years two factors have radically altered the design cycle. First is the acceleration of collaborative communication through technology. Web and phone apps accelerate the design process among team members doing the work, and also with prospective customers (and their contacts) during testing and rollout. What used to take a year or more to design and then a year or more to be talked about in trade magazines and passed on by word of mouth can now attain 25,000 users in a month if there's the right buzz.

The second paradigm shift is a direct response to the increase in ability to communicate and distribute—a more agile, iterative process. The best example of this is the Agile (with a big "A") Software Development movement, which is very specific in describing its practices, yet ironically also emphasizes "one size does not fit all." If you are interested in the specifics of Agile, you can refer to: http://agilemanifesto.org. For our purposes, it's enough to understand that by doing work in small (one- to two-week) cycles and taking advantage of the ability to put these features out quickly to get feedback, the design process is streamlined.

The importance of this was first explained to me by Agile guru, Damon Poole. To simplify the explanation consider the "old way" of doing software development. Once a year a product was released and let's say it had four new features, say that two of them were a mistake and nobody cared about them. In this scenario after twelve months you begin to see value from two new features.

If your development process became more agile, you could instead do four releases, one per quarter. In this case say the Q1 release had a good feature, Q2 a useless one, and the same for Q3 and Q4. Now when you look back after 12 months, you have a very different picture. The same four features are out in the wild but customers have been putting the first good feature to use for **nine months and the second good one for three**.

The big message is **"Get something out there now, get feedback, and adjust. Repeat until people are willing to buy it."**

Of course it's common sense to me writing it, and to you gentle reader, but this is often where the Product Marketing function goes astray. The most common problem here is the Ivory Tower Syndrome. After a couple of successful products have been launched, it's much easier to create products around the conference table with fellow employees rather than to build prototypes, test them, take them out in the world, and get feedback from actual users. The Syndrome intensifies if the bureaucracy is designing a product that its members would never actually buy. In these cases, the opinions being tossed around the meeting room are literally worthless—they have no impact on (or basis in) reality. A leader must arise to seize these moments to break through the bureaucracy and become the product champion. If the team is sitting around the boardroom table, and you are the only one with feedback from 10 customers, you will be surprised at the power you have amassed, regardless of your position on the organization chart.

In many cases, the sad truth is that as long as a company has a few cash cows to milk, everyone is happy with a two-year design/release cycle. This fills everyone's calendar with appointments, the paychecks keep flowing, and life is good (until the cow dies, for whatever reason).

Three steps can assist the Product Marketing Process:

1. Listen: Gather Data
2. Choose Your Adventure: Write a Marketing Plan
3. Work Pragmatically: Cover All the Bases

PMP Step #1 - Listen: Gather Data

You now have the tools to amplify your ears more than ever before. Leverage all the technology you can to gather feedback rapidly, classify it as useful or irrelevant, and begin the next iteration. Regardless of your industry, there is a huge amount of pre-existing data. Using search engines and setting up an RSS feed reader to gather daily reports of your standing searches yields significant market insight. The best part about this kind of passive surveying is that there's nothing to blow your first-mover advantage. If you are actively surveying people and soliciting feedback, word gets around. If you are collecting feedback from the millions of blogs and news outlets, you remain in stealth mode.

As the content explosion continues with social networks such as Twitter and Facebook, this ground only gets more fertile.

For a more active approach, web-based surveying tools such as SurveyMonkey rapidly simplify feedback solicitation from large groups of people. Send your product to 20 people, and then send them five questions. Five cycles of this approach can gather more feedback than many teams can get in a year. This is the kind of approach that can give you a 10-month advantage over everyone else.

PMP Step #2 - Choose Your Adventure: Write a Marketing Plan

"You're gonna need a bigger boat."
- Martin C. Brody

Any time you enter a market, you will face competition. The first challenges that come to mind are similar products in the market. If you are selling Pepsi, you face Coke. Dell, HP and Compaq face off in computer hardware. In some ways, the simplicity of direct competition is a blessing. Indirect competitors, meaning substitutes or alternatives that will prevent your customer from buying are more common and much more difficult to combat. Markets where you compete against "do nothing for free" make head-to-head pricing comparisons a potentially insurmountable challenge. Your targeted plan to meet the specific needs of customers and defeat the competition is the path to success.

There is a chicken/egg problem when determining your market strategy. When will you create your statement of "We will sell X to Y because they need Z"? Before you begin work on the product? After you've managed to sell a few? For smaller or straightforward businesses this may never even be written down. Things like a full cement truck are self-explanatory (people who need cement are the ones ordering the truck). Larger organizations may spend months writing the strategy before even thinking about who would make the product or what will go into making it.

The Marketing Playbook by John Zagula and Richard Tong is a great book to help focus your plan. In their parlance: To examine your market, you review the A, B, and C, and then you examine the P & Q to create your XYZ.

Your Vision of the World – Getting from A to B

Industries arise around gaps that need to be filled. On one side of the gap is the present day, the "A." On the other side of the gap is what life could be like, the "B." The canyon to cross between the two is the "C"—people buy things to throw into the canyon so they can cross to "B."

Henry Ford saw that cars were the future of transportation before most of his customers knew they existed. He lived in a time when cars were expensive to purchase (here's the "A"). He envisioned a future where every family had at least one car (and here's the "B"). His solution was to make cars more efficiently so that they would be cheap enough for the common man to afford (Henry's "C"). Figuring out what problem you solve begins to put your Market Strategy in focus.

Mass Market vs. High Service (P&Q)

The P&Q is the price/quantity trade off (quantity more often referred to as volume). Many markets have high-end solutions, products sold in small quantity at large prices, and low-end solutions, products sold at low price (and often low margins), but in large quantities to still be profitable. Determining whether you are going to do a mass market product or work with one customer at a time, and doing the math to make sure you remain profitable are crucial in developing your Marketing Strategy.

What's Your Value Statement?

Your plan focuses your effort. Having a simple statement at the core makes it easy for everyone in the organization to stay on target and be effective in the use of his or her time. Zagula and Tong cut the value statement into X, Y and Z: We sell (X product) to (Y market) to solve (Z problem). Having a strong XYZ statement becomes the basis of your communication plan and will be the core of the messaging for your product.

To return to Henry Ford – He sold X (a mass produced automobile) to Y (people who had not previously been able to afford one) to Z (allow people from every household to travel farther and faster).

At this point if you have A,B,C,P,Q,X,Y and Z blanks all filled in, you've got the bare bones of a plan. If you are the only solution for this market then you are ready to get to work. For many products though, this is not the case, odds are you have some competition in your marketplace and you need to decide how you are going to face them. The important part here is that by determining a general strategy of how you are going to deal with competition you set some guidelines as to the most effective way to use your limited resources.

Again we return to Zagula and Tong for 5 ways to face the competition, each with risks and advantages. You'll have to select the one you think your odds are best with.

1. Drag Race
2. Platform
3. Stealth
4. Best of Both
5. High-Low

Drag Race. You take the competition head on. Everyone loves a showdown at high noon so it's easy to sell this one to management. The problem is it's expensive and most times there's a winner and a loser, no middle ground.

Platform. This strategy is only available if you have dominated your market. Your next step is to build a fortress to defend your advantage against those who dare take you on.

Stealth. Staying small and nimble allows you to serve markets the big guys don't know about, or can't move fast enough to reach. The key here is to avoid direct confrontation, never challenge goliath or you may get crushed. This is a popular technology play—small startups slowly gathering customers by offering a superior product and doing little or no advertising or other marketing communications. By the time they are big enough to be noticed, a bigger fish acquires them and adds them to the solution set.

Best of Both. In some markets, buyers are forced to make a decision between two options. The best of both means coming up with a new product or service that changes the game. Think about buying tires. For the most part the buyer makes a tradeoff between performance, comfortable ride, and low price. You can buy tires that do one of those exceptionally well, two of them pretty well, but no tire has all three. Coming up with a revolutionary tire material that does all three would be a "best of both" play. Taking this strategy is betting everything on the product. You are gambling that you have a solution that changes the game, and nobody else can match it. You are either going to take all the chips, or you'll be the next Betamax.

High-Low. This technique is for organizations that can handle multiple products; it's a natural defense against the Best of Both strategy. In the event that people aren't really interested in a middle-of-the-road product, you invest in a high-end solution (expensive/powerful/premium priced) and a low-end solution (cheap/bare bones/good enough). Zagula and Tong give examples of hotel chains that offer 5-Star properties and low-end motor lodges to get the majority of market share. On the software front, enterprise products command enterprise-level pricing, while single-user versions can be priced under $100 to capture the rest of the market.

PMP Step #3 - Work Pragmatically: Cover All the Bases

The teachings of Zagula and Tong allow you to write a basic battle plan, and is a superb choice if you are an entrepreneur or don't have a huge bureaucracy to wade through. If that's not the case I would direct you to Pragmatic Marketing. Their Pragmatic Marketing Framework ™ http://www.pragmaticmarketing.com/prag matic-marketing-framework gives you a huge list of items you can cover in a comprehensive marketing strategy. Their framework leaves no stone unturned and covers every possible aspect of both strategy and tactics.

Any comprehensive plan will at least touch on every point of their exhausting framework, a full grocery list. Check out their website for the full diagram but just to give you a sample: Market Problems, Win/Loss Analysis, Competitive Landscape, Product Portfolio, Product Roadmap, Pricing, Profitability, Buying Process, User Personas, Status Dashboard, Customer Retention, Launch Plan, Lead Generation, Sales Process, Presentations & Demos, and others including over 30 items on the diagram at the time of this writing.

As someone who has worked with smaller, more entrepreneurial organizations, I have never done a product rollout using a complete Pragmatic Marketing Strategy. But no matter how small or large the product, at some point in the creation of the plan, I pull out their chart and evaluate each section to see how it applies to the situation and check for anything that has been overlooked.

Not Ready for The Never Ending Battle—Some Pitfalls

One last point on product rollouts. In most industries, products are eventually rendered obsolete by new versions or entirely new products. A common mistake here is to think that you can roll out a new product and still maintain the profitability of the earlier version by not marketing to the existing customer base. This rarely works. In simplest terms, if you are not ready to market to your existing customer base, you are foregoing the simplest market to reach and serve. The rule of thumb is not to expend any sales/marketing resources until you are ready to sell to your existing market. For more detailed explanation of the reasons behind this phenomenon read *The Innovator's Dilemma* by Clayton Christensen. The fact is that if *your* organization has to choose between two paths of what to sell or market, a well-run competitor will always find the cheaper and more profitable path. Christensen's "dilemma" is that new products or research and development are always on the more expensive path. Long-term payout of future market dominance by a better product is not as important as a string of profitable and predictable quarters, so a "well run" company will never innovate. It's not uncommon for organizations in this situation to create an entirely new team and end up selling against themselves. This seems counterproductive, but the only alternative is to cede ground to a competitor.

One of the biggest mistakes I've seen in marketing plans is not taking into account the replacement cycle of a product. It doesn't matter if you see an opportunity to grab 40 percent of a market if the buyers there purchase once every 10 years (enterprise accounting systems for example). A 40 percent opportunity might make an interesting business plan, but grabbing it at 4 percent a year for 10 years is not something the average venture capitalist is going to get excited about (unless it's huge money—say, enterprise accounting systems).

Action Items and Summary of Key 1

Big Ideas:

1. The greater your product is, the less work it will take to market it.
2. Use an iterative process – Try. Adjust. Try again.
3. Create a marketing plan. Define your A, B, and C – What is the world like now (A), How can you make it a better world (B), and How does your product get your customers there (C).

Leveraging Technology:

1. Use online survey tools to gather data about product functionality and user experience. Gather all the data you can.
2. Any technology that speeds up the design cycle, such as web-based collaboration tools directly affect profitability.
3. The same tools you use during product development to gather feedback can be used every time you upgrade the product.

Applying to your CRM System:

1. Don't look at your CRM system as a way to capture contact data about your customers, collect contact data and anything you can about how they use your product. Do they use the product once a quarter or five times a day? Which ones have the technical skills to give you specific feedback? In the design phase you need to identify people that can provide honest feedback that matches what you will see from prospects when you go to market.
2. Make sure your CRM system is a way for you to collect usage data, or at least tag records that have problems with the customer. When it is time for you to improve your product you'll know who to talk to in order to prioritize fixes and new features.
3. Use CRM to gather data to validate the programs you've outlined in your marketing plan. By eliminating ineffective marketing activities based on data from your CRM system you will be able to move these resources to the programs that are working or to test out new ideas.

Key Point #2

Telling the World:
Marketing Demand Generation

Strategy:
There's No Business that's Not Show Business

"The accumulated knowledge of how the Net used to work when it was *difficult* is of no further use now that it is *easy*. This has a curious effect on employment patterns and career paths in high technology. It may be no advantage, or could even be a disadvantage, to have twenty years of experience, because that experience probably relates to an obsolete technology."
– Stephen Segaller, Nerds 2.0.1 – A Brief History of the Internet

With the product taking shape, the next step is to determine the best way to communicate the value of the product. The goal is to make it as simple and straightforward as possible, and to communicate the reason why this product has to be bought RIGHT NOW.

The first challenge you face is awareness. No one can buy a product if they don't know it exists. Thankfully, this problem is much easier to solve than it was before the days of the Internet. Before the web you could easily be waiting 10 years for a message to spread by word of mouth across the globe. Sure, some of those mouths were on network television, which has serious reach, but even then, there was no guarantee of hitting your target.

Today, thousands of unmet needs are being poured into search engines, everything from where's good pizza near me, to how do I hire a private jet for my vacation. This paradigm shift of the common man being able to ask the market for literally anything is the catalyst for the phenomenon of inbound marketing (a phrase championed in no small part by Hubspot and its founders Dharmesh Shah and Brian Halligan – see their book "Inbound Marketing: Get Found Using Google, Social Media, and Blogs).

Regardless of your opinion on inbound marketing destroying all outbound efforts, the fact remains that any outbound efforts are difficult to track and are all a variation of sitting around praying that you make your offer at the exact moment when a prospect is looking for something. Inbound traffic is the true pulse of the market and takes considerably fewer resources to capture. But how they are handled after they show up on the doorstep is now a critical function.

Telling the Story

"All Marketers ~~Are Liars~~ Tell Stories" – a book by Seth Godin

You have to tell the story of your product. This may seem simple, but like many things considered common sense, they are rarely common. Most companies make the mistake of thinking that their product is the story. The worst babble on and on about what their product is. Some are a bit smarter and talk about how they are better than everything else out there. The key is to continue to rise above the details. Part of this is the *Start With Why* – talking about why you do what you do gives customers the ability to identify with you and tell if what you and your product is about is what they want for themselves. This process of identifying with the seller is what generates the trust for the buyer to lay down their hard earned cash to begin a relationship.

To eloquently explain why you do what you do, you need to be an effective storyteller. Giving prospective buyers the ability to see what their life will be like when they buy your product is the key to successfully communicating the value that you believe they are willing to pay for.

Do not explain the product. **Appeal to emotion**. A DVR does not record TV shows, it lets you experience your favorite shows on your own schedule without missing an episode. The mp3 player is not a portable media storage device; it's the magic that lets you keep "1,000 songs in your pocket." Purchasing is motivated by the emotional state the buyer wants to reach. I have a stack of unwatched DVDs in my bookcase at home. Yet every time I go to Best Buy, I am caught up in the fantasy of a quiet night on the couch watching a fun movie. I've finally convinced myself that I will not buy any new movies until the pile of unwatched ones has vanished. Although I have come up with a reason to discourage my purchasing, my emotional state has not changed, I still consider buying a DVD every time I am in the store. By the time I reached the editing stage of this book I completed the unwatched pile of DVDs. Only 10 YEARS after my last DVD purchase.

A good method to get beyond the "what" you do to the "why" is to use the "Perfect Day" method. Many great sales people use this method of storytelling on every sale. Instead of explaining the features of the product you sell, tell the tale of what the user's life will be like after they have the product. Consider the following example:

What: The X-200 is a multifunction vehicle that can adapt to any terrain or weather condition. With more wheel base than any SUV on the market it scores highest on skid-plate tests and is recommended by Fuel Guzzler Digest as the SUV of the century.

Perfect Day: It's an early April day in New England, yet still, it is snowing. Eight inches of snow line the roads. You've seen 4 cars in the ditch on the side of the freeway and one fender bender. You continue home in the X-200 with no concerns about your two kids' safety in the back seats.

Who cares about the market-leading vendor and their awards? Who doesn't want to be the confident and happy driver ruling the world from the front seat? Never get bogged down worshiping the product you've made. Tell glorious tales of what life is like once you own one.

Tactic: Start With the Blog

In the beginning it was all about the website. You had to have your URL and message up as soon as possible. As sites become so complex that it was no longer feasible to manage static web pages, content management systems (CMS) were created – systems that held a database of the website content that was called upon every time a page is requested. This fixed a number of problems – database technology has been around longer than the web, so it's easier to have your CMS automatically update the content, set up queries to look for old or broken content, etc. There's also benefit to the Webmaster, often database forms, or web forms that fill the database are far easier to fill out than writing HTML or PHP code.

Things are changing again as blogging software advances to a point where it's simpler to use and more functional than many content management systems (notice the marketing strategies in play–the high-priced content management systems for enterprise customers versus the low-price blogging platforms for millions of users). Since the technology of the web is changing rapidly, the advantage of having a gigantic customer base allows blogging platforms to test features and functions and roll them out far faster than the CMS industry is able to innovate.

So enough of the history lesson and description of the terrain. What does this mean for you? Although it's not incredibly simple, it is far easier now than it was even 5 years ago for someone to set up a blog and use that as their entire web presence. With a basic template, it's not unthinkable to have a website up and running in a week that's good enough for your first year of business.

Whether or not you should host your own website is still a difficult question with no right answer, but you should review the key competencies of the business and how much IT load you can reasonably take on. The tradeoff is that if your website is hosted on a third- party service, you will have less control and perhaps not have full access to all of the analytical data generated by the site. On the other hand, running a website is not a trivial activity, much like wearing a pink monkey suit into a biker bar late on a Saturday night and trying not to get into a fight. You'll have a lot of people throwing things at you, you won't understand what's going on most of the time, and you'll have a hard time moving around.

The key is to look to your customers. Will you be talking directly to people because of the nature of your product, or are you building a machine that will collect orders via the web and have as little human interaction as possible? If you are running a face-to-face business, then it might be easier for you to outsource a lot of the headaches of keeping up with a website. On the other hand, if the majority of interactions are going to be online, you are probably going to need all the data you can get your hands on, so you'll want to be in control of the servers.

Don't loose too much sleep over this decision, although it can be incredible painful day-to-day if you lose your website. In the long run you can jump back and forth between hosting and in-house in months without a ton of pain. Of course your goal is to set it up once and leave it alone for as long as possible. But it can be changed if you must.

Getting content up on the web as soon as possible will allow you to start measuring what kind of inbound traffic you are getting. Does the copy on your website pull in the right search phrases?

The blog can serve the same purpose. At the very least, resolve to blog at least once a week profiling a problem that you solve. In a perfect world these would be case studies of your customers, as a new business you may be writing use cases of the customers you hope to get. This activity will help you refine your messaging so that it evolves into what the customer wants to hear, or better yet, is actively searching for. As the number of posts you write continues to grow, you will find topics that draw more traffic or perhaps even comments than the average. These are topics that naturally drive traffic, and if your product and messaging align with these, your acquisition cost of new customers will be about as low as it can get.

Tactic: Email – Part 1: Getting Started

"Reports of my death are greatly exaggerated"
- Mark Twain

Looking through the prism of messaging and market strategy it should now be obvious that any new social network that comes along will probably make some bold statements about its ability to finally put email in its grave for good. As long as social networks continue to evolve at a breakneck pace, email has no real worries. Have you checked your MySpace inbox recently? Been hanging around Second Life at all? Yeah, neither have I.

Once you reach a point where you want more traffic than inbound provides, the next logical step is email. Email is the most cost-effective marketing tool having a one-two punch of massive adoption and a wide array of tools to send your prospects and customers clear, concise, and relevant information. Testing your messaging against people who are unaware of your product and not actively searching will give you a lot of actionable data. The Holy grail is to find a compelling subject line that separates prospective buyers from the rest of the herd. Most often this will be related to your elevator pitch - the story you'd tell a prospect if you only had about a short elevator ride to do it.

Where to Begin with Email

The most common approach to email is one of two tactics: transitioning an existing newsletter to email or standardizing lead generation offers. The newsletter is a direct translation of what used to work on paper, and it is outdated. Many lead generation offers are just the next generation of direct mail copy.

It's probably best to use material from both of these sources. As part of your marketing plan it should be easy enough to extend the newsletter concept. Instead of making a company newsletter – often something like a 4-page photocopied list of short articles – you'll break these messages into smaller, more focused chunks of content.

The first order of business is to understand what your readers want to read. Shooting single-shot offers leads readers to unsubscribe after one or two messages. Or worse get you spam blocked–yes, there really is something worse than cold calling. The path to success is to go low pressure and take the time to get a better picture of your readers. Once you understand what readers want, you may take a "hard sell" approach, because you will know that your audience consists of rabid fans waiting with excitement for what you are going to offer next.

A limited-time offer for a limited edition science fiction movie action figure will be considered spam by 99.99% of the world, but there is that 0.01% who will wet their pants when they get your email. You want to get to these people without antagonizing the 99.99% so much that Gmail refuses to send your messages. To build your list beyond names and email addresses, the first few emails should be either surveys or newsletters that have multiple topics so you can get a better feel for what's popular and what your readers have no interest in.

This is the chance to tell your story – unfiltered and pure. Unfortunately this is a double-edged sword. You no longer have to worry about a reporter or editor spinning your quotes to fit the story they want to tell, but on the other hand, you are now responsible for growing your own audience. Major newspapers and TV networks have this covered when you ride along with them; now it's going to be your responsibility – and guess what? If your message isn't interesting, they will run away.

Knowing you have the intestinal fortitude to not fear that statement, we continue on.

If you have an existing newsletter, you are going to want to change your approach. Rather than the standard fire drill ("OMG, we need a newsletter this week, let's get 5 stories!"), go with a less stress-inducing approach. Go to your blog, where you already have a content calendar churning out an article a week. Once a month, bundle up the blog posts into a single email and send it out.

Now, instead of doing the classic newsletter, you've got a blog doing some of your SEO (search engine optimization – helping the search engines find you) and opening up a channel of communication. You also have content being generated on a regular basis and can check your email software (or your web analytics, if you are not using an email tool) to see what topics resonate and where the opportunities are.

Note: email should always come from a person's name, not "Acme Widget Newsletter." It's usually a good idea to be consistent with the subject line – "Acme Widget October News." These are only guidelines though. You'll want to test these things yourself. More on that later.

It is also a good idea to have short article summaries that link to the content rather than the entire stories. Many studies have shown that readers tend to scan for the interesting stuff, so it's in your best interest to use bulleted lists and minimize scrolling. Plus, if you give all the content away, you are not going to get that great click data you need to learn what stuff the audience values most.

Getting Your House List in Order

Every house list (the list of emails that you own, as opposed to a rented list) must start somewhere. The trick is to start enhancing the data you have. Once you have first names, most email systems will allow you to address each outgoing message individually. You would add something like #firstname# to the copy of your message and the system will plug in the correct data. (These are called merge codes.) Many tests show that using the person's name in either the subject line or the body copy can significantly improve results.

House Lists usually fall into 4 types:

1. Paper list (thankfully heading toward extinction).
2. Text file.
3. Excel spreadsheet.
4. CRM solution.

We will ignore paper lists. Text file is the most basic and least powerful way to go. They get unwieldy even after 100 entries. On the other hand, text files (commonly named .txt or .csv, the latter for "comma separated value") are often the preferred format for importing and exporting lists from system to system. Excel works well, but tends to fall under the old adage "If the only tool you have is a hammer, every project starts to look like a nail." Many people do things that Excel was never intended to do, just to avoid switching to a real CRM system.

Beyond that point, you have a few options. If you are only doing email for outreach it's best to manage the list through your email service provider. If you also need to share data, access with other parts of your organization. such as your sales force or accounting department, I am biased toward Salesforce.com. The idea of having access from the web and having someone else manage the database is appealing (there are plenty of other solutions out there too, including ZohoCRM and Sugar, as well as a number of enterprise level solutions).

Managing the list consists of these activities:

- Removing dead, invalid or unsubscribed contacts.
- Appending new information to contacts as necessary.
- Examining to determine what information should be appended.
- Adding qualified contacts.

For your first communication, you have to decide how to send it. It is possible to just use your personal email account, but this doesn't scale very well.

WARNING! Do not make the mistake of taking a whole list of addresses and putting them in the "To:" field. You really don't want anyone to be able to hit "reply all" and cause a lot of trouble for you (or forwarding it to your competitor). Many people will fill in the "To:" field with their own addresses and put everyone else in the "bcc:" (blind carbon copy) field. This is a little suspect too. Legend has it that it will brand you as a spammer, but I think the more important factor is whether you have prior established communication with your readers. If not, the bcc tactic may keep some of your messages from going through.

Professionals get a vendor account, and there are some free options that work well enough for a small community group or a family. While the principles of email are simple, the vendor selection process can be quite complex.

The basic steps:

1. Load up your list. Usually a simple process. Go to a web page, select the text file or spreadsheet that has your names, and then you can usually find a confirmation page that shows how the data will be mapped (i.e., Is column 1 the first names? Is column 3 the email addresses?). You may also want to add a few Seeds to your list. These are email addresses of your own so that you can confirm that the message went out. It's a good idea to have seed addresses for the HAMYs (Hotmail, AOL, MSN, Yahoo – and we'll add Gmail) so that you know that your message went through everywhere, and you can use the same addresses for proofing your message to make sure it looks good on all the big email services and in email client programs.

At this level even basic email systems must have 3 functions:

1. They should disregard and report back to you on invalid emails in the list.
2. They will not allow duplicate addresses (under no circumstances should a single email address be sent the same message twice).
3. Addresses that are already on your "Do Not Email" list should be disregarded. They may be less than happy with you, and antagonizing them won't help.

2. Prepare your content. The subject line is undoubtedly most important. Because you are sending using a person's name in the "From:" field, it's not going to look like commercial email. This is a good thing: you are trying to do person-to-person, not unknown behemoth-to-person. Your reader is going to try to decide if it's compelling enough to open on the subject line alone.

Also at this stage, you don't need any crazy graphics. Keep it simple, using short paragraphs, bulleted lists, scannable text, and some links so you can track how it does.

3. Proofing. The most critical part. Once you have it set up, send a test message around to your seed addresses so you can confirm that it looks right and that all the links, including unsubscribe, work properly. The worst possible industrial accident you can have in email is sending out a bad link. Not only do you have to either fix it with a redirect or eat it as a failure, you'll also have to answer all the really polite messages telling you only idiots include dead links, thanks for wasting my time, and oh by the way, where's the unsubscribe link, that better not be broken. **Don't do your own proofing**. This is a marketing best practice. The person who writes copy usually has a difficult time editing it without missing things. When you write something, you tend to gloss over the copy and miss mistakes you have made. Always have someone else read over your copy to make edits. There's always some person in your organization who's a world-class editor. But it can be a challenge to find that person. A service like ProofreadNOW.com will be happy to assist you.

Pulling the Trigger

"I love the smell of napalm in the morning."
- Lieutenant Colonel Bill Kilgore

Sending the message is the scariest part of all. Everyone has at least a twinge of doubt when he or she clicks the final "Are you sure you really want to send this?" button. At that point, it's like ringing a bell. There's no un-ringing it after it's done. Although it can be a harrowing moment, there are no documented cases of a marketer suffering any lasting physical injury from an email blast. Well... except for that big time spammer who was killed by the Russian mob.

Once the send button is hit, the fun really starts.

Email is a direct descendant of the direct marketing field. For non-marketing people, direct marketing (or DM, for those in the know), is basically mailing stuff – catalogs, credit card applications, etc. It's always been a profitable venture, but often considered the uglier cousin of the glamorous world of advertising, especially TV. For a DM professional, email is like crack cocaine. In the past, the DM people would send something out and then wait 3 weeks for something to get mailed back. In email, your diehard fans (and unfortunately the unsubscribers) will start clicking almost immediately.

Many a marketer has spent his or her afternoon checking the results page on an hourly basis to see how high the open rate and click-through rates will go. Once you get into testing (the next section on this tactic), it's like running your own horse race. In no way do I condone gambling, wagering on results, or forcing co-workers to do unnatural acts if their subject lines don't perform as expected (but I do understand it).

Afterblast

Your email may have a long life span. You have no idea when your readers will open it. All the following figures are averages based on what we've seen – but you need to test these for yourself.

Every market is unique. Usually, more than half of the opens will come in the first 24 hours, and by the end of the next Monday (after busy executives finish their weekend email box cleanup and those off on vacation the previous week return to the office), you've probably seen all the action you are going to get, with the exception of people who do things like quarterly email cleanup or have folders of stuff they look at only on holidays.

The concept of an **email half-life** can be helpful in analyzing results without having to wait months to close your stats. If possible, you want to track results on an hourly basis for the first 24 hours and then daily after that. One month later, look at your stats and determine when you had half of the total number of opens. This time point is your half-life, and for most people it tends to occur in the first 24 hours. Comparing half-lives gives you some reliable stats on a faster basis.

The First Things to Track with Email

- Open rate. The percentage of sent messages that were opened (either manually or possibly by the preview pane of the email client)
- Bounce rate. The percentage of sent messages that could not be delivered
- Unsubscribe rate. The percentage of recipients who asked to be removed from the list. (Some email systems separate complaints from unsubscribes, as they are different).
- Click rate. The percentage of opened messages that had readers click through on a hyperlink, excluding unsubscribers (Note: It looks more impressive to management as a percentage of the number of opens, not number sent).
- The links that were clicked. It is critical to determine what is hot or compelling.
- The number of conversions (sales, sign-ups, whatever...). Your return on investment (ROI) – is this worth continuing?

Good luck and happy hunting!

Tactic: Email – Part 2: Intermediate

"Have you got anything without Spam?"
-Mrs. Bun

You have experience with email and are using tools that make you more productive. Your messages are of the highest quality. If you are beyond beginner, doing basic email, like a monthly newsletter, and want to kick it up a notch, this is for you.

The Art of Email (and Marketing in General)

Email, like all marketing, is both art and science. The problem is that we are usually telling a story to convey our enthusiasm for whatever we are talking about and trying to encourage others to act. Unfortunately, the human decision process is far from rational (some would argue not rational at all), so no matter how many stats you measure, there will always be an X factor that you cannot account for.

Our testing methods may be scientifically sound, but we are not able to control much of anything about our human recipient. The difference between a click-through and getting spam blocked could have something to do with the failure of the reader's prune juice working that morning, and this is nothing you want to have any input on.

This is the "marketing as surfing" analogy: every day and wave is different. We use the tactics that work and improvise as we go. The good news is that we don't need the full scientific method. The method of testing discussed in "Tactic: Email – Part 3:Expert" would never be used in the pharmaceutical industry without validating the results of the test. However, we can presume that our results are close enough and fire away as soon as we think we know what the optimum combination of factors might be.

Autoresponders

An autoresponder fires an email usually triggered at one of two times: after a reader takes an action or after other criteria have been met (perhaps downloading certain files from your website). It's a best practice to have an autoresponder set up so that when someone signs up to receive your email, you fire back a message confirming that they have opted in. You might also send your last message or a welcome message with some of your greatest hits – content that you have tested and know to be world class.

Depending on your offer, autoresponders are also a good way to validate recent sign-ups. If you are giving away a promotional offer, such as a white paper or some free music, you can have it hosted on a web page. But if you set up an autoresponder instead, now you know that the email addresses you get will be deliverable, as opposed to the mickey@mouse.com address that tends to show up in a lot of promotions.

Testing

The holy grail of the direct marketer is testing! Once you can deliver a message out the door without Herculean effort, it's time to start testing. The most common is the A/B test – take your list and randomly split it into two lists. One group gets message A, the other message B.

The idea here is to change only a single variable, and subject lines are a good one to start with. From personal experience it's not uncommon for one subject line to be 4 to 10 times better than another. In this case, aside from the subject line, everything else is the same. It has the same body copy, sent at the same day and time, and all links direct the reader of the message the same pages.

When splitting the list, you must be careful to use a method that is statistically reliable. One of the best ways to do it is to sort by recency of the email address (how long they have been in your database. Older email addresses have a higher probability of being dead) and then tag them A and B sequentially. Otherwise, if you find out that the average age of the B list is 3 months less than the A list, you've probably already tipped the scales to the B list side. If you don't have the recency, it is a good idea to sort by company name so that if you have 40 readers from the same company, they get both messages.

What to Test?

Listed in order of importance here are 3 areas to test:

1. Subject lines (If they never see your offer, it doesn't matter).
2. The offer.
3. Everything else, primarily deliverability or things that affect the open rate.

Subject Line

The subject must be compelling. Answering the "What's in it for me?" question is always a good exercise. There's also a long-standing debate about the effectiveness of using "FREE" in a subject. Although many say it will hurt your deliverability and move you to the spam side, I've found that the benefits to conversions outweigh any deliverability concerns. Your mileage may vary.

Commercial email systems allow you to use merge codes in the subject line (as in "Hey #FirstName#, do we have a deal for you!"). As a general rule, anything you can do to make the message more personally relevant is going to improve results. If you have that feature, play with it.

Like many facets of email marketing, best practices are constantly changing. There have been many "best practices" about the benefits of graphics, and long subject lines, or very long emails that may or may not apply to you. Believe what you test, not what some bozo preaches in his book on marketing.

On the other hand, many vendors now take this into account and use an email format that includes both a text version for handheld devices and a full-blown graphics version. Again, test all of it.

Other Variables to Test

Copy. Short vs. long, bulleted vs. paragraphs, the offer itself.

Graphics. Intangible products can get by without graphics while things like fashion or jewelry simply cannot. If you are using any images, this will require you to be able to use whatever HTML editor your email service uses. For the most part these are WYSIWYG (what you see is what you get) editors with lots of word processor–style buttons on the top command bar.

Most systems will also let you add raw HTML, in case you have some talent there or a web designer to help you out. Layout falls into this area also – one column, two columns, three columns. You can even get crazy and go with a horizontal scroll, a look that shows up occasionally for the fashion industry.

Time of day. Get to know your readers and think about when they have time to read. A better email system will let you see the opens on an hourly rate – if you see that they all get opened after 5 p.m., maybe there's no point in sending before noon. Early sends are worse because your message is buried under everything else that comes in before 5 p.m.

You should avoid "email crush time." For business, anything sent after 5 p.m. on a Friday will probably end up in the huge pile of email that the reader returns to on Monday morning. It's better if your message comes in alone at 2 p.m., rather than being in a stack of 100 Monday morning emails, worse yet, a stack of 800 if the reader has been on vacation during the last week. Sending at noon may put you in a small pile of "after lunch" email, as opposed to coming in alone at 3 p.m. Of course, if your readers view your message more as recreation, the time frames are reversed. Anything from 9 to 5 Monday through Friday will be part of crush time on a personal email account. This can also happen in business for senior executives who clean up email on the weekends. More than one business test has shown better open rates for senior executives on the weekends than during the week.

For all the above, don't forget to pay attention to time zones. Ultimately you should have enough geographic data to figure out where everyone is. An email sent in New York at 10 a.m. will be fine for the East Coast, but it will be buried in the stack of morning mail for everyone 3 hours behind in San Francisco who hasn't come into the office yet. You may want to consider doing separate blasts for other parts of the world that are more than 8 time zones away. Better email systems will allow you to schedule the outgoing messages so you don't have to get up at 3 a.m. to send your message off to Japan. Email throttling is a tactic that can be used to determine the best time of day to send. This will be discussed later.

Deliverability. This is where things tend to get more technical. Overall, deliverability is a black box problem. You have no idea how AcmeCorp has its email system set up. It could be just a straight pipe going in, or it could go through a third party to filter out questionable or unknown senders, and may even go through a second internal system to remove any blacklisted senders. Regardless, there are plenty of things you can do to improve your deliverability rates.

Checking for bad addresses is one step you can do prior to loading. Tools such as Advanced Maillist Verify can use a "handshake" to contact the server that gets your mail and confirm if the address is still valid. By removing dead or invalid email addresses, you increase the deliverability rate of your messages, which, in theory, gives you a better email reputation because you don't have a lot of bouncing messages.

There are a number of different standards that can increase deliverability, such as SPF (Sender Policy Framework – www.openspf.org). Large services like the HAMYs use their own standards that must be met. The easy solution to this problem is to use two email service providers to do an A/B test with the sender being the only variation. If you see no problems, you are probably in good shape. If one beats the other, you can take that up with the vendor.

Another concern for deliverability is the health of your IP address. This gets into the heavier tech side of how email gets delivered, but the short version is that the system that sends your emails has a unique identifier (something that might look like 168.120.34.2). Many systems that track email senders use these codes to identify mailers. There are two issues here. One is that your email provider may be using the same IP address for multiple mailers. The problem is that you may be sending great targeted, relevant messages that people want and some bozo sharing your IP address is sending online casino garbage (or worse). In these situations, everyone on the IP address can get blocked.

This can be avoided by getting a dedicated IP address. Many mailers offer this, but often at an additional charge. The good and bad news here is that you have responsibility for the IP address. Behave well and you may get deliverability rates above and beyond the norm. Do a poor job keeping your lists clean (not removing unsubscribes and bounces, buying lists from snake oil salespeople on the web), and you may find yourself at an address that has burned out.

If you are in the big leagues, over 100k being sent on a regular basis, you would probably want to work with an auditing firm that specializes in deliverability. Services like ReturnPath can take this work off your hands so you don't have to worry about what every ISP is up to.

Frequency. How often to send is one of the last things to test. When you reach this point, you probably have a stable of strong messages that have tested out well and now are focusing more on how often they can be sent and how to get more readers to scale it up.

The easy answer is to ask someone how often they want to hear from you, but testing shows that's not always the best thing to do. As mentioned earlier in the Art of Email section, humans are irrational. When asked "How often do you want to get email from us," readers tend to underestimate; once a month is a common answer. Some tests in certain markets show that you can easily send twice a month and get the same performance (but you are now doubling your results). In general, when we make long-term plans, we tend to over-estimate our ability to get bored.

In practice, many readers go through a natural progression of consuming a lot and then tapering off. This fits well with trying to learn more about your readers. You can send weekly and learn about what interests them the most, and then taper down to only the content you know they are interested in. In general it's usually best practice to sign them up for everything but always give them the option to manage their accounts to opt out of certain types of messages and reduce the frequency to once a month or per quarter even.

If you've made it to this point, you are now looking at your email campaigns as a whole, probably not worrying too much about individual messages but instead focusing on the life cycle of the customer. When do customers show up? What are they interested in at first? At what point (if ever) do they begin spending money? Email has become an effective tactic for you, and you're probably spending more time worrying about the readers themselves.

Tactic: Email – Part 3: Expert

It's no longer enough for you to just get the message out. You are at a point where squeezing out an additional 1 percent can be the difference between getting that fat bonus check versus just making your number, or you are integrating the results of your email campaigns into other services such as customer relationship management (CRM) or marketing automation tools.

At this level you've probably been doing email marketing for years, have some battle scars, and have scaled up completely. Things get a bit different here because of the sheer volume.

For example, the average 20,000-message mailer (with a slightly less-than-average list) is looking at maybe 2,000 opens; meaning 200 click-throughs to get to 5 conversions. If this guy is selling $5 widgets, that's $25. This guy is not going to pay $50,000 to double the results.

On the other hand, Joe's Obnoxiously Expensive Products is sending 2 million messages a shot and giving away some good stuff to a well-qualified list. It gets 800,000 opens for 100,000 click-throughs for 1,000 conversions. Joe knows his customers have a lifetime value of $10,000, so you're talking about $10 million. This is just a 1% increase, which means $100,000 free money (or $100,000 toward the most incredible email and CRM systems you can buy, so you get to go to the President's Club event in the islands that usually only the sales guys go to).

The Message Is More Than One Message: Taguchi Method

In the expert scenario you live and die on testing and you can afford the infrastructure to do multivariate testing, often referred to as Taguchi testing in email marketing. Taguchi testing, also called multivariate testing, is a simplified application of the work of Genichi Taguchi, engineer and statistician.

With a large enough list, you can test multiple variables at the same time. There are a small number of email vendors that support this level of testing, and there are many consulting services that do this type of work.

When doing A/B testing, most people think "splitting the list," 50 percent A, 50 percent B. Actually, you only need to send a certain number of messages to get results that are statistically significant (there are a number of calculators on the web, but a good rule of thumb is to have more than 40 responses, which on average would require about 5,000 sent). In other words you can do an A/B test that is 90 percent A and 10 percent B and still have statistically valid results. Multivariate testing takes this one step further.

The idea behind multivariate testing is to build a matrix of all the variables you want to test and send enough of each so that every test is statistically significant. Here's an example:

	Graphic Set A	Graphic Set B	Graphic Set C	Graphic Set D	Text Only
Subject Line A	2%	-4%	5%	1%	-4%
Subject Line B	8%	5%	12%	3%	0%
Subject Line C	-7%	-15%	-2%	-9%	-10%
Subject Line D	2%	2%	10%	1%	-3%
Subject Line E	0%	-1%	3%	2%	-1%

This test runs against 5 different subject lines and 5 different graphics sets. By taking advantage of this type of testing we are able to effectively run 25 separate tests at the same time. In the example above we can see that Subject Line B and Graphic Set C is the most effective combination, but more important, if we had tested independently, the odds are that our lift would only be half as much (you're goin' to the islands, baby!). The idea of doing 25 tests at once makes it much faster and easier to find out what works, but the challenge is cutting your list into 25 separate segments and managing all 25 versions of the message. This is possible manually. But also remember that to keep your results valid, it is best if they were also all sent at the exact same time and date. This is a lot to ask of a manual send, and that's why for this stage you'll probably be looking for a powerful email service provider.

It's important to note that **Taguchi testing can be just as effective for websites and AdWords Analysis.** You can get better results faster with these techniques.

Throttling

Most basic email systems just fire away when the trigger is pulled. That may not necessarily be in your best interest. Some IT departments watch the inbound mail to make sure that no one domain is pounding on the email list (especially if a lot of them are bouncing). A more advanced email system can stretch out the send time over hours or even days so that deliverability improves. One interesting thing here, this tends not to be a benefit to "spammier messages". It gives community vote systems, such as the one Gmail uses, more time for messages to be tagged as spam and not get delivered.

The ultimate in throttling is its combination with automated Taguchi testing so that a test can be run on a smaller portion of the list and the email system itself can select a winner when it has enough results to be statistically relevant and fire the remainder of the list with the best possible message.

CRM Integration

When you are running a large-scale operation, you can get a lot of value out of direct integration from your mailing system with your customer relationship management (CRM) system.

The goal is to be able to alert a salesperson whenever someone responds to an offer. At the very least it should be set up so that any conversion notifies the sales representative. Beyond that, it depends on how busy your sales team is and how willing they are to qualify leads. After conversions they may want to look at the clickers that did not convert to see if any are worthwhile.

WARNING! When you set up reports for representatives to see these, be sure to filter out the unsubscribes (not all clickers are equal). If reps want to dig deeper, you may want to record opens also. Reporting everything that has been sent is a lot of information that you may not want in your CRM system. It's better to keep track of them by campaign (for example, if you set up a series of 5 emails for everyone who currently uses AcmeWidgets, you probably want to just tag it as a member of the Acme campaign, rather than add 5 "message sent" records).

There are two levels of importance here: one is to record the history so that it is in the customer record, the other is to **push alerts to the sales team**. This is commonly done via email alerts, or pop-ups on more advanced CRM systems. A low overhead solution is to set up a weekly email to all reps with a link to an existing report in the system. Not as good as real time, but at least it gets the job done.

Website Integration

There are different degrees of integration depending on what you need. At a bare minimum, your web analytics should be able to tell you how much traffic your email is generating. On the other end, high-end CRM or marketing automation systems can monitor your website so that web traffic is also recorded in the customer's record, and email campaigns can be kicked off based on specific pages hit on the website. These types of campaigns can be extremely successful because they are so narrowly targeted. If someone has come back to your site 3 times to download a certain type of white paper, you can be sure that if you send them a fourth, they are probably going to check it out.

These create the holy grail of understanding your customers, the unification of web analytics to see what content they want, marketing automation to see what email messages they respond to, and the CRM system so their entire history with your organization is recorded. Failure to reach this level is the source of the customer service issues that many large organizations face. Marketing doesn't realize it's pointless to offer the new product because the client is fighting with the support line about the existing one. Or another classic example - getting transferred to another branch of a company and having to start over at square one giving your name and account number again.

Effective Surveying

There are many resources on this topic, and doing it well is beyond the scope of this book, but it deserves mentioning. Surveying readers via email is a great way to get a lot of data into your CRM system without much manual labor. The idea is that you get a list of 15 characteristics about them, give them something of value in return for answering questions about these topics, and then have a much more detailed view of these people.

This can be done in one shot or, if you are more adept, set up as part of a metacampaign (more on that later). Once you have this information, you can take advantage of…

Lead Segmentation and CRM Integration

As your understanding of the readers gets to be more accurate, you can use fields in your CRM system to keep track of specific facts about the readers. By knowing more about what they buy, how they use the product, and all sorts of demographic information, you are able to send more targeted messages on specific topics that will guarantee better results for individual messages.

For example if you have a new product that helps cars run better in cold weather, being able to exclude from your mailing list any states where the average temperature never goes below 40 will significantly improve your results on a percentage basis and avoid burning out email addresses on the list that will definitely find the offer irrelevant.

Lead segmentation can be turned up another notch with...

Lead Scoring

Lead scoring is the evaluation of the quality of a lead and the creation of a corresponding point score so that it can be judged versus other leads. This can get very complex, quickly, and is discussed in depth later on.

Metacampaigns

Metacampaigns are setting up series of interactions with prospects. These are sometimes referred to as "email tracks" or "drip campaigns," but they do not have to be limited to email. The most advanced mailing systems will allow you to set up processes that run continually. For example, if a person fills out an info request form on web page X, they get the information via email. They are then sent a follow-up message one week later to see if everything is working as expected. A month later the person can be sent a link to a video that shows how successful customers use the product in ways that new users might not have thought of.

Metacampaigns are only limited by your ability to understand your customers and their behaviors during the sales cycle, their life cycles as customers and your imagination. You can use this approach not only to extend email to its maximum value, but also to test other mediums beyond email. Having touch points here for things like social networks or mobile communications and applications will allow you to effectively test what your customers use and want to communicate with. You never have to jump into the next tactic (like social media) cold. You can systematically test your options and have some certainty about what will work.

White Papers

"Consistency is the last refuge of the unimaginative."
-Oscar Wilde

Once your messaging starts to solidify via the website and email campaigns, you can start to write more advanced material that backs up your compelling statements. Your content generation strategy is still focused on the written word for two reasons: first, text requires far less effort than audio or video content production, and two, the amount of search engine impact in exchange for the labor to create the content is highest with text (audio is more expensive to produce, video even more so).

There is an entire spectrum of written work that you can do beyond the web page. Prior to the advent of the web a "White Paper" had a specific meaning. It was often a technical document, more of an academic publication than advertising vehicle. A typical white paper might be 15 to 40 pages, very dry, and often vendor neutral. With the recent content explosion there's now a full spectrum of sizes and formats for company generated content. At one end of the spectrum, there is value in going beyond the white paper and doing an entire book. Many firms have found great value in being the ones "who wrote the book" on a specific topic. This also makes a pretty impressive business card for the author(s), and can provide access to speaking engagements and other events that a company would either have to pay to be associated with, or may have no other access to.

At the other side has been the creation of the eBook, often a PDF document fewer than 40 pages, set in a landscape orientation for easy viewing on a computer screen, and optimized to spread rapidly online. Creating some quality content that is either free, or requires sign up is the realization of *The New Rules of Marketing and PR*, the earliest and most successful book to forecast the transition of Marketing and PR to become their own publishing house. There's often discussion as to whether or not this content should be behind a registration wall and there are valid points for both arguments. On the "frictionless" side is the fact that it's not uncommon for a white paper to spread to more readers in a full order of magnitude greater than content behind a registration wall. On the other side is the reality of lead flow to your sales team. The team is faced with one of two situations – they are lead starved, and will jump on anything that could be a lead, or more commonly there's a huge backlog of leads that have never been contacted by the sales team in any way. If you have a backlog, the idea of getting 12 qualified names sounds a lot better than having to sift through 1,200 that will just get thrown on the pile.

Are you trying to get your message out to as large an audience as possible to generate awareness, or are you looking for some qualified leads to pass to sales? This will drive your decision about how to distribute.

The Content

Written content will fall into three categories:

1. Explanation of new practices or theories.
2. Case studies of successful use of new practices or theories.
3. How-To Articles.

All three are useful, and some would say just a variation on the same theme: education. But by using one of these three methods your readers will have a level of comfort with what they are getting and how it will be presented. Take advantage of the readers' familiarity and desire that compels them to read, for example, "The Top 10 Pitfalls to Avoid When Doing X." Entire publications have been built around the how-to and case study content models. You can literally go into any market space, start producing content and be guaranteed traffic if it is relevant and written in the marketplace's "native tongue."

Using the Hype Cycle

News and media outlets have been courted, sponsored, wooed and everything else by the business community for as long as people have been paid to spread the news. A huge portion of the PR industry has been built around promising better access to the mass media channels, whether it's network TV or mentions in the Wall Street Journal. The promise of access to a large market has always been a shiny object to the businessperson.

The problem here is that every corporate marketing or public relations person worth a dime will believe that every single thing done at their company is not only interesting and compelling, but also market leading. On the other side is the person that has an audience who wants news of some kind, and who will make an editorial judgment usually along the lines of "Your company has something interesting to say once every two years at best." Corporate communications people need to stop drinking their own brand of messaging, and start thinking more along the lines of "If people had to pay to get this content, would any of it sell?" There's also opportunity if you understand how the media responds to new technology over time, also known as the Hype Cycle.

The first step is to understand the media. My *Marketing Over Coffee* co-host, Christopher S. Penn, has a simple method to do this – take a look at the magazine rack in the supermarket checkout. Here you will find the headlines that compel people to buy right at the point of sale. Many of these have been refined over decades and deliver results on a regular basis.

At this point, many marketing people are unable to look beyond their own sense of self-importance. Anyone putting out a press release about version 8.5 of their product that believes this could go toe-to-toe with "The Top 10 to Ways to X your Y," some celebrity getting divorced/married/having kids/dying of cancer, or anything to do with tasty looking food, or boobs (at least to half the market), is overestimating what the market is looking for. News outlets want controversy, human interest, deception, and other compelling Shakespearian topics – not the kind of stuff you see in almost every corporate press release: "The market leading blah blah blah announced version of blah blah blah. Executive 1 said: "insert generic quote here", Executive 2 said: "second generic quote", company boilerplate.

Always connect to something compelling. One angle is to connect to something topical, but this can often be a stretch. Using the latest boy band name in your marketing literature may get you some new clicks, but for the most part, it's again a huge parade of worthless names. The key is to latch on to a hot topic on the way up.

Gartner, a company of analysts that spends a lot of time analyzing different markets, has come up with a model called the "Hype Cycle" that does a great job explaining how topics tend to get hot in the media, fall off, and then vanish, or return if they are able to survive the marketplace.

As any topic gets hot, it will continue to spread at an accelerating rate through the population. Often, just like any fish story, it will continue to expand with every passing to an exponentially large group. Once it reaches maximum expansion, the hype will have grown to the point where a smaller group of people will question the importance and power of the story - often the seed group that found out about the topic in the first place, who are now bored with it or experienced a shortcoming of the product or idea. This results in a plunge off the radar as fast as it rose. What was a hot topic in the last news cycle is often the punching bag for the next. It will continue to fall until it is forgotten entirely by the media and its survival is left to the marketplace to determine.

That last point is critical – survival is not determined by the media and its hype cycle, but by customers that vote with their dollars in the marketplace. Podcasting is a great example of the hype cycle and the market in action. As the technology started to get hyped up in 2006 it continued to accelerate for over a year. Podcasters were being featured in newspapers and on TV news. Soon the bubble popped and podcasting was old news. Events dried up, many early adopters moved on to Twitter or other social media shiny objects. The numbers in the marketplace tell a different story. The listening audience has been growing by 20 percent annually for years. It's also started to look much like all other media channels – a small group of producers hold the majority of the audience. Although there is more diversity than ever before, people tend to congregate around a small group of the most popular producers of high-quality content.

With this understanding of how topics move along the hype cycle, you can adjust your strategy accordingly. There is a huge first-mover advantage if you jump on a topic as it begins its run up the curve. If you are an early expert you'll be called upon to explain the new technology to the masses, and get plenty of free publicity. This will continue as long as the technology is hot. If you jump in second or third, you can still do well, but your results will be an order of magnitude less than the first movers. The most common mistake is jumping in near the peak. There's always a point at which there are a number of "experts" in the new market, but few successful case studies to convince the laggards. This is when the "get rich quick" crowd joins the innovators and the press and public tire of the hype. You will see this point if you watch the media outlets closely and start to hear and see things like "How to protect yourself when choosing an X vendor" or "Results from X technology not all they are cracked up to be." Calling what the public believes to be "The Next Big Thing" a fake or fraud is just the kind of controversy that sells papers.

Now the descent begins. The early adopters fail to see huge returns and move over to the next shiny object. The press is tired of the topic and it falls off the public radar until the point where a killer app is created and the new technology is put in their hands.

Attempting to get any publicity at this point is usually a lost cause. This is when you become your own publisher and tell the tales of your successful customers. This is the weeding out period where the people who are delighting their customers with great results will have the reserves to ride out the down cycle and all of the wannabes will fail or move on to something else.

Eventually the value of the product will survive long enough to silence the naysayers, or it will fade into oblivion. It can fail at any time, but the two most common failures are that it languishes or fades at the bottom of the trough, or at any point in the curve it's replaced by something that renders it obsolete by being better, stronger, faster, or easier to use.

Another worthwhile set of concepts to understand for this transition period, and for the product marketing cycle are those created by Geoffrey Moore in his book *Crossing the Chasm*. Besides the predictable cycle of the media's response to a new technology, there's also a predictable pattern to how it will be adopted by consumers.

Mr. Moore explains that there are two markets for a new technology that matter – the early adopters who are the first to buy the products, do interesting things, and tell the world (which helps feed the ascent up the hype cycle), and then the mass market that sees the value in the product and comes out in droves to buy it. The key point here is that the two groups are different in their purchasing criteria. The early adopters are thrilled by the new technology and are used to having to do a lot of work just to get things to work and understand that early versions of products may fail frequently and need some babysitting to keep running. The mass market on the other hand does not tolerate failure and is not willing to take any time to read a manual or learn how to use a product. For mass-market success you want to be no more complex than an on/off button, if possible.

Knowing where you are on the hype cycle allows you to get a feel for whether or not you will be able to take advantage of existing hype, or if you should focus on generating your own content because that's the only hype you are going to get. Knowing where you are in relation to the chasm helps you understand if your message should be aimed toward people who are willing to do some extra work to get things running, or if you need to refine the product so that it's simple enough that anyone with a room temperature IQ can make it work.

The New PR

"We overestimate the impact of new technologies over the next 2 years, and underestimate its impact in 10 years" – Bill Gates

"I haven't seen a PR shop that would get out of bed for less than $4K/month" – Mike Troiano

Advertising and PR Agencies have been powerful tools to generate business. Over the past 10 years there has been much uncertainty and discussion about the future of the agency.

As the impact of "everyone as content producer" is absorbed by the marketplace you have writers/bloggers saying you can get by without PR people, and you have marketing gurus saying you don't need the writers/bloggers. You're the expert in the space. You can create your own content. Why work around some other pub's schedule, or spend time bringing a journalist up to speed on your specific niche when you can publish your own stuff and own the content, track it, and do with it as you please?

I believe that as agencies become skilled in the digital arena they will continue to thrive as the "junior staff leverage" model is proven (a small group of experienced, well-paid people that manage a large group of inexperienced poorly paid serfs that do the majority of the labor).

PR is about developing a broad communications program that includes:

- Building a long-term strategy that establishes lasting relationships with your core audiences;
- Creating content and managing conversations that engage those audiences directly; and
- Reaching industry influencers (media relations gets lumped in here).

Tactically this means that the communicator or agency you hire should have skill sets that include: writing ability, audio and video skills, creative thinking, and the ability to connect with influencers.

This sets up a prediction for what the agency of the future might look like. Most marketing, PR, and ad agency positions that revolve around tactics will be reinvented – this a either a huge opportunity or tragedy based on your perspective.

The big idea is **the Embedded Agent**. Someone who can go into an account a day a week or more to shoot video, record audio and create other relevant content. Ideally they would be paired with a subject matter expert (SME) at the organization who will ultimately speak on behalf of the client. Think about building your own Robert Scoble (when he was the Microsoft evangelist) or Scott Monty at Ford. This forces a schedule of content production that can be used in a number of scenarios and at the same time will boost search engine results.

The position of Producer/Editor (or Preditor, because that sounds really cool) who assembles the raw footage from the agent is an important position. Preditors have access to the best tools and a support network of their peers – no client would be able to reproduce the effectiveness of the Agent/Preditor team, so this is a huge value add. This team would need an administrator to handle scheduling as the agent will be moving around a lot (let's say with a three-client load), and the preditor needs long stretches of uninterrupted time for work. Somebody needs to field calls and emergencies.

Beyond the teams is the infrastructure that the client has access to that cannot be reproduced without huge expense by the client – the remainder of the value add. These are audio/video production and photography, specialists in a variety of disciplines including CRM, lead generation, and whatever the agency can leverage that clients need.

Influencer is the last category, executives that have access to people with markets. You can get on the *Today* show? Clients will pay for that. Having a strong database here would allow this system to scale to multiple people instead of a single performer limitation.

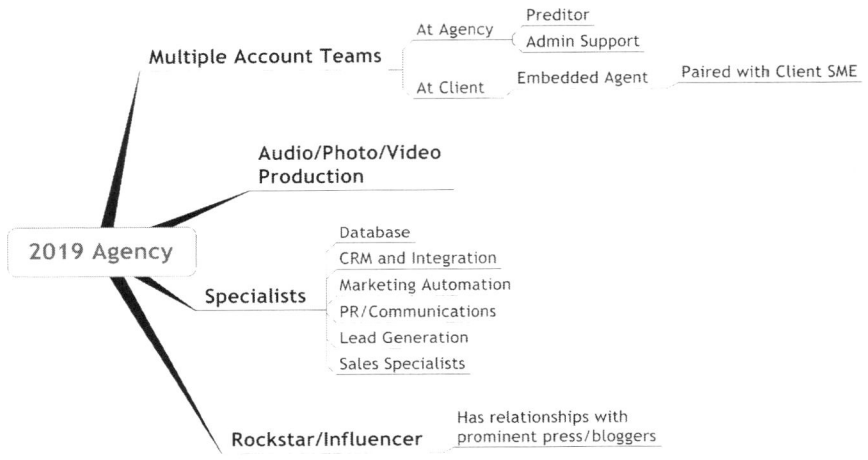

An Agency FROM THE FUTURE!

OK, enough with the prognostication, can we back solve this to a profitable business?

A Team would cost around $370k per year in salaries (including benefits, taxes, etc.):

- Fully loaded agent – $200k
- Preditor $120k
- Admin $50k

Divide that $370k per team by 3 clients and you are at around $123k in expenses. Charge the clients each $150k ($12,500 per month). The client is getting more than one third of an agent and preditor at just over the cost of the preditor. And they avoid the impossible task of trying to hire one-third of an agent and preditor. All the specialist stuff can be sold ala carte for big margin.

Direct Mail

"Facts do not cease to be because they are ignored."
-Aldous Huxley

Direct mail has been (and still is) a huge market. Although I have used these tactics many times in the past, I believe that it will continue its decline, but never go away entirely. There's always some value to sending a person a gift, but the economics have shifted away from this being the low-cost method of getting to the mass market. The Internet has taken its place as the cheapest way to get to the masses.

An excellent book to read for inspiration here is *Ogilvy on Advertising*. His discussion on creating effective prose is as relevant today as it ever has been.

Just as a technology's popularity can rise and fall, marketing tactics (for the most part becoming technology-based) rise to popularity and then fade, yet many never completely die. As Chip Griffin once told me when I was predicting the demise of newspapers "Remember that there are some people that still listen to AM radio." We will always have candles and people writing letters, but these become personal expressions, not the cheapest/easiest/fastest way to do things. Remember that the personal expression is more likely to start a relationship with a customer. Figuring out how to do that cheaply is the art.

Like any other marketing tactic, it lives and dies on testing. The only hard part about testing is that there is no "right" answer because the target is always moving. The things that delight customers go in and out of fashion and all you are doing by testing is trying to catch and ride that wave.

For direct mail there are two categories that can be effective. One is the mass-market mailing such as catalogs, brochures, and simple offers driving traffic to personal URLs (sometimes called PURLs – unique web addresses for every piece so you can track what hits). Many times the goal here is to go as cheaply as possible. The more pieces you can squeeze out of your budget, the more leads will show up. Although this method is expensive (writing a check to the post office for a quarter million dollars is often putting your job on the line), the quality of your mailing list can make this a great way to do business. It can also be effective with existing customers where you can target the mailing toward items you know that they are already purchasing. These projects run in two stages – producing the collateral and then getting it into the mail stream. Organizations that market this way often have designers on staff as well as outside professionals that they use to create the mailings. Once the design is completed, a mail house of some kind is often used for high volume mailings. These vendors handle the printing and get the mailing into the mail stream.

There are three methods of tracking that can help in this high-volume bulk-mailing environment. First is tracking codes or personalized URLs to see which pieces are effective. As you get into this world there are hundreds of variables to test (just as in email), and if you have the volume you can do multivariate testing here too. Cover images, color, number of pages, copywriting, time of year to mail, barely scratch the surface of the infinite variables you can test.

A second system for tracking is the use of seeds. Having addresses in your mailing list that go to people you know will allow you to confirm the time it takes to ship and the condition that the mailing arrives in. There are companies that provide this service. They can give you a list of seeds from all over the U.S. and then they will batch them up and send them back to you. This can be useful if you are trying to target the landing dates for your mailings (so your mail doesn't end up like the candidate mailing which arrived at my house the day after the election). It will also show you if you are having problems with boxes or low-quality paper that arrive looking like, as Redd Foxx would say, "The funny papers after the kids got through with them."

The third important system to have in place is closing the loop with bad addresses. In a perfect world you would have a system set up so that you could process all of the returned mail before you do your next mailing so that you are not sending out a $1 per piece mailing to an address you already know is dead. The key here is making it as simple as possible to handle the data entry for the mail that has been returned. At the very least, you could place the ID code that the prospect has in your database somewhere on the mailing so that the person processing the return only has to enter a 12-character code instead of having to look up the address. If you are doing huge volumes of mail you might consider some form of barcode scanning to accelerate the data entry process.

The other direct mail option is to go for a high per-piece mailing. The idea here is to send something fairly expensive that cuts through the clutter – a hand addressed large box, sometimes called 3D mailings that will make it past the mailroom to the desk of the decision maker. These can run into problems because they can be expensive. Others will view them as outright bribery depending on the value of what you are giving away. Hopefully, whatever you are sending is related to your product somehow so that it's not just giving away the latest hot gadget, but is something that has a real connection to what you are doing. For example, if you were giving away some hot multimedia device, if it was preloaded with videos of your product in action, that could be effective. You could also tell the prospect that if they are unable to accept any kind of gifts they are welcome to ship it back to you, or better yet, call your local representative and he/she will stop by to pick it up.

Another effective tactic to reduce expenses is to try the "Something's Missing" mailing. I once received a box from Oracle Software that was about 12 inches by 18 inches. On the lid of the box there was a picture of a yacht and when you opened it up there was a cardboard cutout in the shape of a set of binoculars. The call to action was simple: set up a demo and get the binoculars. In fact, economics of it were fantastic: sending a bunch of $5 empty cardboard boxes, while getting the impact of giving away some expensive ($100?) binoculars. Better yet, instead of mailing a thousand of them, you only have to purchase enough to cover the ones that convert to meetings – probably only 1 percent to 5 percent of the total number sent. That's a huge savings. This can be replicated many ways: sending cheapo earbuds instead of mp3 players, sending photos of items instead of heavy hardware. Get the impact by effectively telling the story to everyone, without spending money and shipping expensive stuff to the whole list – just the real prospects.

Surprisingly, I've found that direct mail can still be effective but the weakness is in the time it takes to determine the failures. If I send a batch of email out I know by the next morning how many of the email addresses are bad and these are sent off for cleanup or removal from the database. When a batch of mail gets sent out the whole list goes off to sales for follow up, but it can be weeks or even months before the "return to sender" packages start showing up. At that point we already know they are bad because sales has tried to contact these prospects that are no longer at that address (most likely moved on to something else). Again, we are drawn back to list quality – if you've got a fairly clean list this is a great way to do a remarkable campaign that drives traffic. If not, you are better off going a cheaper and faster route to clean up the list before you start spending a lot of money.

Trade Shows

"There are moments when everything goes well; don't be frightened, it won't last."
-Jules Renard

Trade shows and other live events have been a cornerstone of promotional activity since the dawn of business. Regardless of developments in technology there is no more accurate way of assessing customer relationships (or potential customer relationships) than face-to-face discussion. As long as there is any evolution in a market there will be a need for the participants to learn and discuss the changes they face. There are many technologies that can provide much closer to an "in person" experience, but none as effective as getting hundreds of people together under the same roof.

Defying all common sense, the biggest mistake made with trade shows and other events is not having a clear plan why you are there. Smaller organizations are usually better than large ones in this area. Small companies need more business and at some point end up saying, "Let's try this event to get more business." Larger companies have often been doing an event for years and there's little discussion as to whether or not they should be there and it's often viewed as a chore (or worse yet, punishment) for the folks lower on the totem pole, forced to confinement at the booth for the entire event.

Although there may be some arcane reasons for your company to attend an event, there are three that are the most common:

1. You understand that the attendees match the profile of some of your profitable customers, so it stands to reason that talking to attendees would beat randomly picking titles out of some list or phonebook.
2. You can take advantage of the fact that you have prospects and/or existing customers that attend the event. Instead of a sales guy getting on a plane 10 times over two months they can meet with all 10 in one trip. This is the same reason many attendees go to these events, instead of evaluating 20 vendors over two months of coma-inducing conference calls they can wander the show floor and talk to them all in one day and pick up a wide assortment of trinkets that are in the middle of their lifecycle from the Far East to the Landfill (stress ball anyone?).
3. You are expected to be at the event. Some conferences have so much momentum in the market that if you've been at one of them for many years, if you were to skip it your competitors would rapidly spread FUD (Fear, Uncertainty, and Doubt) about your financial

stability. Regardless of the true risk of not attending, nothing motivates like fear, and large marketing bureaucracies rarely see the need to give up budget unless there's somewhere better to divert it to.

When you have determined why you are going to the event (and have a list of the goals you will accomplish such as meet X number of new leads, have Y worthwhile meetings with existing clients, run a session with Z number of attendees), the big question is "What to do at the event?"

Please don't make the same mistake everyone else makes of having a booth that looks just like everyone else's, staffed by people who don't really care to be there (or worse yet, don't know much about what your company does). I've found it useful for the first year of considering a show to go as an attendee so that you can get a feel for the event and the quality of the attendees. It's also a good idea to bring your camera and take pictures of the show floor to see how most of the exhibitors present themselves.

Once you have decided to have a presence at the show, the first order of business is to find out where on the show floor you will be. There is a complete spectrum of the amount of leverage you will have in this process. For most events, you have a fair amount of leverage when you are negotiating to be part of an event. For most shows, the exhibit hall still has some available space, so there's no reason for you to pay the rack rate to be part of the show. In fact, many events have media partners or nonprofits that they will trade floor space to. The marginal expense of the smallest booths in the back of the floor is next to nothing. One trick here – you may be shown a floor diagram of a full exhibit hall. Usually this is misleading; often there is at least one wall that is just a curtain that can be moved back and forth to make additional rows as needed (but showing a full floor gives the exhibit sales team the first taste of some leverage).

A brand new show that has never been run before will have no leverage and will be working hard to get new exhibitors. Depending on your tolerance for risk this is the best time to strike a deal. You'll get the best price and the exhibit sales people will not forget that you stepped up when needed and will often continue to give you your preferred rate even when a show begins to take off. This reward is subject to risk though because many event management companies will sell what they can and will not make the decision to kill an event, that doesn't have enough interest to happen, until a few weeks prior to the day it's supposed to happen. You can structure your deal to get your money back, or strike an even better deal on the next one, but neither of those makes up for the leads you won't get this quarter.

If you were really clever you could set up a deal so that if the show didn't go off, you at least could get the lists that they promoted it to, or perhaps a chunk of their house list. Don't tell anyone I gave you this idea.

This leads into another point that you should dig into as you are evaluating the show. The most valuable asset of any show is the attendee list. Many events use this as a leverage point. Exhibitors over a certain class are often entitled to the attendee list, which can come in a number of flavors from a list of mailing addresses at the low end, to full attendee detail including email both prior to an event and afterwards.

At the other end of the spectrum are the big time established shows. These are huge shows that bring tens of thousands of people into the cities and are able to put the squeeze on the exhibitors. The magic happens for the exhibit sales staff when the show floor is full, and they are able to select venues that keep it full every year. At this point the prices tighten up and there's often incentive to sign up for next year's show while you are at the current one. It's not uncommon to have your sales rep set up an appointment for you while you are at the show to go to the show office and check out a large map of what next year's floor is going to look like so you can pick the plot you want.

At the exhibitor's weakest position there is usually a point scale set up so that exhibitors with seniority (having had a booth for multiple years) are entitled to pick from the limited stock first.

There may be all kinds of rules behind the scoring system, but it all boils down to the fact that the people who have spent the most money get the most points and first shot at the good stuff.

Once you have decided to do the show, you have to select an open booth. The most important criteria here is to try to understand the traffic pattern on the floor so that you are at a point where most of the exhibitors will at least walk by you once. There are only two ways to get this right. One is to do a site visit ahead of time. This can be cost prohibitive and not completely accurate as every show can choose the floor layout, so what might be a central aisle for one event may be a dead end in the middle for your show. The only sure fire way to get this right is to roll the dice on the first year and then you'll know what to do for year two.

Another easy thing to do is check the entrance and bathroom locations, which are always busy. Larger venues will have food vending areas that will be busy at lunchtime. Be sure to check with your exhibit sales rep about the schedule of events for the show floor. There may be an amphitheater having sessions that will have traffic, or better yet, there may be meals, appetizers or cocktails offered on the show floor during exhibit hours. I've seen many of the cheapest booths on the floor get crushed with traffic when the caterer sets up the beer cart right next door at 6 p.m.

Once you have your own little plot of real estate selected, the next step is to figure out what you are going to do with it. A common configuration is to have a backdrop of some sort with your signage on it, and at least one station with a monitor so you have something more interactive than just the posters behind you.

There are two things that drive your booth configuration – your goals for the show and the experience you want visitors to your booth to have. Note that this is contrary to what the majority of companies do. The average company has no defined goals for the show, and is worried about the booth properly reflecting their branding. As a result, most of the booths on the floor are so boring that you won't even be able to tell one show from the other. Besides the crime of looking completely stock photo boring and exactly like everyone else on the row, many companies somehow manage to do even worse by giving their representatives some chairs and a table so that they can treat the booth like their cube for the week, not only showing the disrespect to the attendees of sitting while they stand, but actually having a physical barrier of a table between them. It's only a matter of time before someone sets up a Lucite window with a drawer so they don't have to give out their crappy free pens to everyone (but at least that would be remarkable).

If you don't want to get to the end of an event with everyone asking, "Why did we bother to do that?" decide on what the goal is so you will know if the show was a success or not. Then do everything in your power to make your presence there compelling, interesting and remarkable so that people may actually even want to talk to you, even if it's to hear what the buzz is about.

Ultimately you'd like to have interesting conversations at your booth, so please consider that when you are setting it up. For many shows you will have the opportunity to purchase the carpet for your section of the floor. For less than $10 a square foot (at most shows, remember every market and show is different), you can get deluxe padding under your carpet that will make your booth a destination resort for anyone that has been walking the floor for more than one day.

One of the best configurations I've ever used was a 10x20 foot booth with a normal 10x10 booth on one side and rented curtains to make a little private 10x10 room on the other side. Note that there are show rules that have to be followed and odds are you cannot set up a 10x10 cube that blocks the view to your neighboring booths. The key to doing this is to be at the end of a row or have your own "island" with no neighbors. Most shows allow you to rent all sorts of furniture, so we got a nice table and 4 chairs and had our own little conference room. At a big show where prospects have been walking around for 3 days, you will be able to tell them every story you have about how great your product is and still have to kick them out of the chairs when the next group comes around.

You'll notice that many of the big vendors get this. I've been to shows where huge beverage companies buy 80x80 foot squares and set up a full bar to facilitate discussions. I've also seen booths that have a second floor with private conference rooms where contracts can be signed.

Once you have a rough sketch of what you want to do, you have to get all the hardware together. The biggest mistake you can make at this point is to go to your local exhibit company and have them sell you a booth that you will then have to ship all over the country and find somewhere to store when not at a show. If you are getting started and don't have a lot of budget there are two low-cost, effective solutions. The cheapest and easiest is to get a display shade. It looks sort of like a projector screen, except you set the roll on the floor and then have a segmented metal pole with a hook on the end. You pull the sign out of the bottom cylinder and extend it upwards and hook it on the top. You can get three or four of these that are 2 to 3 feet wide and 6 feet tall for a wall of content. You can also get cheap halogen lights that clip to the top.

Lighting is every bit as important in displays as it is in camera and video work. You can never get enough light. Your signage may look OK without lighting until you put it on a row of booths that have lighting, and then you'll look like the dark and dingy ghetto of the neighborhood. Don't lose the impact of the color and graphics you've spent good money to create by cheapening out on the lighting.

The "retractable shade" method is the cheapest way to go. The shades are light enough to be carried around by your booth staff so you won't have to ship them, pay to have them brought from the docks to your booth space, or pay to have union people set them up if the exhibit hall is a union shop. Shades run between $200 and $400 each so you are talking about less than $1,000 for the look that you want (contrast this to a 10x10 aluminum frame booth that will cost you $2,000 to ship from Boston to San Francisco just shipping, not setup, not graphics, just moving the damn thing). The downside of this method is that the shades take a beating (as does everything involved with trade shows) and you probably won't get more than two or three shows out of your kit. For many teams that I worked with, this is not really a bad thing because it was rare that the messaging on the signage stayed the same for more than two shows in a row. You also have the advantage of being able to have two or three panels that are generic with your logo or other copy, and then creating one or two with messaging specifically for one show or for a promotion that you are doing only at that event.

If you have a few more dollars to work with, many shows offer booth rentals. You'll get a standard aluminum frame booth and then the opportunity to order three or four sign panels that will fit into the frame and make it look like your own. This will often run around $1,500 and often comes as a package with the frame, signage, maybe some chairs and a trashcan (including the service to empty the trash can daily, which otherwise is something you have to file an order for), and electrical power. If you are looking to minimize your headache, or are traveling a long distance, this takes a lot of pain out of the show. You are going to look a little bit lame, especially if you are on a row of all rented booths, but there's no schlepping banners on a plane, just showing up and having it already built and ready to go for you is a big deal, especially if you are doing two or three shows a quarter. The fact that you just walk away when the show is over is also worth some money.

At the far end of the spectrum are the teams that work for large corporations that are doing more than a show a month. At this point, the financial analysis says you should probably own your booth, and maybe even have a company contracted to move it around and set it up for you. The problem is at this level the marketing department has become a huge bureaucracy, so the odds of seeing anything cool or out of the box from these guys is pretty rare. Having one of the big guys creating a purple cow is just as rare as it sounds.

Once you have the hardware design put together you'll spend a lot of time on the signage. This requires strong graphic design, copy writing, and some proven strategies. The biggest mistake people make here is sketching out the booth design on paper and then blowing it up to full size. This design process is a recipe for disaster. You need to take into account what the booth will look like from the aisle and the impact the rest of the booth will have on how it looks. You can tell a rookie design when you look at it on a sheet of 8.5x11 paper and the sheet is full. For most booths at least the bottom third of the space is useless. You'll have a table in front of it, booth staff blocking it, and even your $75 trashcan in the way. Also remember that people need to be able to read the text from the aisle, so if you have a bunch of paragraphs of information on your signage, what you have is unreadable.

A good trick is to go to an existing show, take a photograph of a bunch of booths, then get two or three you like and import them into Photoshop. You can then remove their logos and images and replace them with your own. You'll be surprised how small the amount of space you have to work with is, even when you are working with a 6' x 10' panel.

One common strategy is the funnel design – use large copy and graphics at the top that can be seen from the aisle, then make a second level that's smaller and has more detail to pull the attendee in to the booth if they want to learn more. At the lowest level you can go smaller yet to have graphics that your booth staff can use to explain to attendees when they are talking right in front of the signage. If you have a few dollars to spare you can also use this lowest level to hang a monitor on the display so that you can demonstrate product, show videos, or use interactive content. This works very well because it can be updated for every show and takes up no additional booth space.

With the display completed, give some time to staging the flow of traffic in the booth. Where will your staff stand? If they begin a discussion, where will they move? If they engage an attendee and want to scan their badge or show them more information, where will that happen? Managing the flow of traffic in the booth is important in the first few hours of the show, or during times when there is food/booze on the floor. These are often the busiest hours of the event and you'll probably get 90 percent of your leads in the 10 percent of time that the floor is the most active.

One note on crowd control – the important strategy is to make sure you are not tripping over each other in the booth when it gets fast and furious. On the other hand, you don't want to be so efficient that there's never a crowd at your booth. There's nothing that will bring more traffic than a group of people in front of your booth. If someone is walking down a row and there's a crowd at one of the booths, it's human nature to wander over there to see what's going on. I always cringe at a show when I see a 10x10 booth with a wall of four people (all dressed in the same lame-o polo shirts and khakis) acting as a human shield to keep people away from their booth. Who would want to be the first person to go over and put their hand in that shark tank? You'd probably never get it back.

As a good marketer the first thing to do when you see that is send two of them back to their hotel rooms to put on street clothes. At least that way you could make it look like someone is interested in your booth.

One quick point here – many shows are at venues that have hotels attached to them. Usually they are better quality hotels, cost more and tend to fill up quickly. For really hot conferences it's not uncommon for people to book their hotel for the next year on their way out from the current show. If you have a tight budget, other hotels will be much cheaper, but at the very least get one room at the venue. There are some serious benefits to having a room at the venue. For example, you will be saving money by not having to taxi or drive to the show, which will add up quickly and can be a logistical hassle as everyone tries to arrive at the show floor for the opening hour. You will also have a place where everyone can leave their bags or valuables instead of under tables at the booth, and most importantly, your own bathroom that won't see 1,000 people per hour. Another benefit is that as a guest of the hotel you can have packages shipped there for your arrival such as brochures or giveaways. If you are not a guest of the hotel this can be either a hassle or expensive. You either ship them to your hotel and then have to figure out how the hell to get them over to the venue, or you have to pay shipping to get them to the venue and then pay the exhibit company to get them from the dock to your booth. Going that route, having three or more groups handle your packages is the fast track to an ulcer. Remember that if your brochures are a day late you might as well ship them straight to the landfill.

Once you have everything together there's a bunch of other paperwork that needs to be taken care of (the larger the show, the more likely that this process is all online, which makes it much easier. The smaller the event the more likely there will be paper shuffling back and forth, but this is quickly changing). Along with signing a contract for the space you'll also have to file orders for the carpet, electrical service, Internet service, rental of lead capture devices, depending on the union status there may be labor required to set up your booth or signage, furniture rental, plants or water service at your booth, vacuuming your carpet and emptying your trash, and any specialty stuff depending on the show (at the National Restaurant Association show there's forms to order fridges, stoves, all kinds of logistical nightmares). All of this is bundled up in the "Exhibitor's Guide," a document filled with the show rules and order forms. Fill out all your forms and get them in on time. There are normally three tiers of pricing – you get the best rates if you have your orders in usually about a month before the show. If you order within a month of the show they kick the rates up a bit as incentive for you to order earlier. The worst is if you screw something up and have to order it at the show – prices can be two or three times the early order price and they may ask for one of your body parts (which would probably be cheaper).

The true art of this is crafting the attendee's experience – what are they going to see/feel/hear/be intrigued by? If you are doing things right, they will be caught by something compelling that pulls them to your booth. They will then interact with your booth team to find out why your product is remarkable, at which point they will be offered something that is interesting enough that they are willing to give you their contact information in return for it. If you are doing it right this will be aligned with your sales qualification process so that you come home with a list of people that are the types of folks that usually buy your product as opposed to a list of freeloading people that were interested in free candy bars.

Some things that seem like common sense yet are uncommon on the floor:

Put your product to use. I see no better example of insanity than the events for trade show professionals (people who build and sell trade show booths or manage large events) where the companies that sell promotional items (such as coffee mugs, T-shirts, and stress balls) are exhibiting at these events, but not giving out coffee mugs, T-shirts or stress balls.

Traffic for traffic's sake is better than nothing. I make light of giving away candy bars as that really isn't bringing quality leads, but candy bars are dirt cheap and a crowd is better than the human shield of polo shirts at the empty booth mentioned above.

Shift in to high gear. If you are in the rare circumstance of having a lot of qualified traffic be sure to have a "high gear" that you can shift to in which attendees get a 5-second pitch and you get their contact info to invite them to a future event or give them a promotional item if they take a meeting at a later date. The strategy here is that if you have more traffic than you can handle you want to get as many of them as you can. You don't want them to wait in line for a few minutes and then move on if they get tired of waiting.

Have a reason for people to stop. At the very least, raffle something off. If attendees think nothing's going on at your booth, you are better off staying at home.

Have a well-oiled lead capture system. Make sure you have your lead capture process set up, tested, all booth workers trained on it, and have a backup plan that is also tested and can be deployed immediately. There's no bigger disaster than being in the first crush of traffic and having a badge scanner crash on you. If badge scans are a big deal you will want to get to the exhibitor level where you get the attendee list so that this problem vanishes completely. Until you have that kind of money, your entire show depends on getting every good lead you can when it's in front of you. It might be worth the extra $300 to order a second badge scanner as an insurance policy.

After many years of working shows, there are a few tricks I have picked up that can significantly improve your experience:

1. **If the names are good, get all of them.** Again, if you can buy them, great. But if you can't, don't just settle for everyone you can get to see you at the booth. Odds are that a huge number of attendees are just going to be too busy with other things to find you, out of all the other exhibitors at the show. One killer tactic is to get to know the other exhibitors at the show that are in your same boat and try to work out co-promotional events with them. For example, there's another vendor in a related space that is in the same market that does not compete with you. If you both take your lists after the show and invite them to a webinar and share the resulting list, you can both improve your number of leads and you'll be taking a second step to qualifying them by only talking to the ones interested in your event. This tactic worked exceptionally well for me. For some events, more than half the new deals that resulted for a show were from leads that did not visit our booth at an event.

2. **Keep a first aid kit in the crates.** It's not a show without somebody bleeding at some point. This is not an issue if you have a contractor handling the booth for you. But if you are involved in the setup and breakdown you will definitely get banged up at some point. Trade show crates and exhibit halls are always covered in grime, so you'll want to be able to clean your wounds as soon as possible.

3. **A bottle of scotch is good too.** It's an effective painkiller, and for some events, if you are packing and shipping your own stuff, you may have a lot of time to kill waiting for your return cases to arrive at your booth after the show closes. Also, you didn't hear it from me, because it's probably illegal, but I have heard of people that have traded booze, or cash, to get their cases back faster after the show. I have also heard that there are show workers who say they can do that and will just run off with your booze or cash. Choose the people you trust wisely.

4. **Arrive a day early to set up.** Setting up the booth the same day you arrive onsite is asking for trouble. Odds are there will be some critical parts missing and you want to have enough time to get to the local Home Depot to buy a hacksaw, some clamps and whatever else you are going to need to repair whatever parts were custom made just for your booth and crushed during shipping (bonus – save your self some hassle and have the address to Home Depot in your GPS before you get there).

5. **Always advance ship to the warehouse.** For most shows you will have the option to either ship everything direct to the show floor the week of the event or ship it to a warehouse to have it arrive more than a week prior to the start of the show. There are a number of reasons why advance is better. One is that it can be confusing when you are placing your orders for the show. But it is cheaper to ship advance. Normally you pay a lower rate per pound and the cost of moving your freight from the warehouse to the show floor is included in this price. When you ship advance you are usually charged a lower rate per hundred pounds. This is because it's easier for the exhibit company to manage the logistics of getting everything to the floor if they have it a week in

advance rather than having everything show up at the Convention Center loading dock. Besides being cheaper, there's also the safety net of having some time in case something terrible happens. By shipping early you can call a week before to confirm that all five of your cases are there. If you time it for five cases to go from Boston to Las Vegas and arrive the day before the show and you get there and there's only four cases you may have ruined everything. Lastly, there's the benefit of having the exhibit company store the booth for you in their warehouse. If you do enough shows there will come a point where you could keep the booth in motion from show to show rather than paying to have it stored at your own warehouse.

6. **Bring a box cutter, but always keep it within the show crates.** Bring it to the airport and your next prostate exam might be at 'Gitmo. This actually brings to mind a more important topic – the checklist. I have a standard checklist for every show and you want to use it during setup and after tear down. Make sure one of the items on the list is "Throw all tools into shipping crate."

7. **Save your back and use the empty crates.** If you know what you are doing packing the booth, you will probably have more space in the crates going home than when you went out (with the brochures and giveaways gone). You can save your back by grabbing one of the free bags they give away at shows and put any heavy, non-essential items such as any textbooks from sessions or other promotion materials you've acquired into the cases. I will neither confirm nor deny that I have done the same with my dirty laundry after a show, but you need to do something with all that glitter covered stuff from Vegas.

8. **Don't forget the tape.** Some critical items for your show crate: Packing tape (both duct and the wide Scotch tape used for sealing boxes, black Sharpie – writes on most stuff in permanent ink (many marketing people have an addiction to these pens). It's always a good idea to have a flash drive with soft copies of all show collateral. In the event of a lost box you can run over to the local Staples and get more printed up. It's not cheap but it beats having an empty booth.

9. **Get your bill of lading 3 hours before closing, if possible.** Closing time at the show is a bit confusing if you've never done it before. There will be a lot of cheering when the lights go down and they may even announce over the PA that the show is finished. Although you may be tempted to start packing things up early, especially in the last 2 hours of a five-day expo where you've had no leads come by for the last 2 days, be sure to check the show rules. It's quite common for shows to have penalties for early teardown, such as fines or loss of ranking points for securing booth space the next year. It sounds crazy, I know, but I have seen the show photographer running around an hour before closing to take pictures of people that are blocking the isles with open crates that they are stuffing things into. If you are using a lean and mean "pop-up" style booth, you still might pack what you can get away with and then you tear down as fast as possible to go out for the huge post show celebration dinner (it's common to get a night at a 5-star restaurant after a week of breaking your back). If your booth is being shipped, you have to sit around and wait for your crates to show up before you can pack. This can really suck. It's not uncommon for crates to show up 5 or more hours later for huge conferences. For these big shows you are better off grabbing your dinner and coming back the next

morning in your crummy clothes to take care of it. You will either be issued a bill of lading prior to the show close, or you will be required to pick it up after the show closes. This is a form that usually has four or five carbon copies that outlines how many boxes, crates, whatever you have, how big they are, how much they weigh, where they are being shipped to and who is moving the freight. The rookie mistake not to make is start packing when the show closes then have to go wait in line for 40 minutes to get your bill of lading, fill it out, then go back and wait another 40 to have it signed off on. The right way to do it is to have someone pick it up 3 hours before closing, or if that's not possible, have a team member in line to pick it up when they announce the closing of the expo floor. If you do this right you will be on your way to dinner while the rookies are waiting in line to get their paperwork before they can start packing. Once you have everything packed, you bring the forms back to have them signed off on. You'll get your copy and that's it, you just walk away. It's kind of strange to just walk away from thousands of dollars of gear, but that's the way it works.

10. **Bring a tape measure.** It's not just to measure stuff. Here's a common problem: You get to your booth to set up and you find that instead of an electrical outlet coming up through the carpet in the center of your booth there's just a box of outlets at the back of your booth. You have two options – you can go wait in line at exhibit services and pay the special "ordered during show setup" rate (probably $200 an hour, 1 hour minimum) or you can do what the electrician is going to do when he gets to your booth three hours after you placed the order: Take your handy box cutter and cut a hole in the carpet where you need to have the outlet. Slide your tape measure through this hole and under the carpet until it comes out at the back of the booth

where the outlet is (you may need a co-worker to lift the carpet at the back a bit to slide the tape measure under the rug). Plug in the extension cord you brought in your show crate (always have two extension cords and two outlet strips in the case), and use your duct tape to tape the extension cord socket to the end of the tape measure and then pull the tape measure (with the extension cord taped to the end) back out to the hole you cut. Just like fishing! Note that you don't want to be doing this when anyone is around, especially the electrician or any of the union members. This can be a hazard due to friction on the extension cord from the carpet – make sure you are running it under carpet that is not being walked on. This is kind of risky but since you ordered it that way and they screwed up your order I don't want you to take a $200 hit for that. You can give me my share of the savings next time we catch up for a drink.

11. **Order the padding.** Nothing cooler than having leads want to hang out at your booth just because you coughed up the extra $200 so that everybody could be more comfortable.

12. **Staffing adequately beats good shoes.** Odds are you are dropping thousands on the show so don't cheap out by not getting the padding or doing something stupid like having 3 people work the floor for a 3-day 36-hour run. You should set it up so that people are rotated off after 2 hours and have an hour to get some food or get off their feet. Even on a "light" day of three 2-hour shifts most people get less friendly and visitors to your booth can feel it.

Trade Show Bonus: Travel Secrets

At one point in my career I would be on the road for three out of four weeks of the month, often visiting six or more cities. After one particularly long run of trade shows, I did a blog post on some of the tips I had learned along the way. It proved to be popular and several people contributed some of their tips. Although it's not specific just to marketing, I thought they were worth cleaning up for inclusion here:

1. **Never check a bag.** This is gospel for most business travelers. An airline can't lose what it doesn't have. If you must check a bag, keep a spare set of underwear in your carry-on in case your bag gets lost and you need to go out and buy more clothes. Also, if you check a bag, don't rush to get off the plane. You're just slowing things down and you're going to have to wait at the carousel to get your bag. Enjoy the seat while you still can.

2. **SeatGuru.com.** I was using this long before my friend Chris Christensen took it over (and has since then moved on). You tell it the airline and the type of plane and it shows you where the good and bad seats are. You only have to get stuck next to a high-traffic, high stench lavatory once to make this your favorite travel site.

3. **Bring twice the money, half the clothes.** I believe this one is attributed to Erma Bombek and is dead on.

4. **Only bring the things you will use, not the things you probably, or might use.** For business travel, most of the world has a nearby drugstore or a friendly concierge that can get you anything not on your "absolutely required" list.

5. **Universal charger.** This used to be a necessity for me: a device that replaces a bag of AC adapters with one that can charge your laptop and all your devices (unless your laptop is a Dell, which uses a proprietary charger and I swear to God one day I will find a way to get Dell back for this). This is becoming less of an issue, and if you buy your devices wisely you can

come up with an all USB system so that everything can charge off your laptop.

6. **American Express Platinum Card.** This is kind of pricey, but it gets you into the flight clubs. If you've ever been snowed in at an airport and had to sleep on a bench and wash your face in the public bathroom, you'll appreciate the better clubs that have a place to sleep, take a shower, work on your laptop and perhaps even enjoy some food and an adult beverage (they do have regular beverages too). Getting out of the pandemonium in these kinds of situations can really reduce your stress level.

7. **Get the lightest laptop you can afford.** Buy a second battery while you are at it. Some PCs allow you to use a drive bay as a battery. With two regular batteries and one in the drive bay you can probably get a full work day.

8. **Sit on the aisle so you don't have to climb over people to get to the bathroom.**

9. **Never sit for more than 2 hours without moving around.**

10. **Have a solid 10 to 12 hours of books, movies or TV shows on your iPad or laptop.** You never know when you will be stuck someplace with time to kill.

11. **At home, have a second set of toiletries ready to go.** You never have to pack and see what's missing. Leave the bag in your wheelie cart and go.

12. **Kayak.com for comparing a large range of departure times, airlines, and prices.** You tell it where you want to go, and you can adjust the results to show you arrival and departure times at every leg, reduce layovers, etc.

13. **Priceline.com for hotels.** I'm consistently paying half what other guests pay. For flights, I don't have the flexibility of traveling at any time, but the hotel I stay

in is a different matter. There's no faster way to learn a city than to stay in as many hotels as possible.

14. **Always have a small flashlight, Sharpie, and business cards.** A tiny LED light can solve a lot of problems, as can a permanent marker. Although we are nearing a post-business card age, odds are you'll meet the power exec that wants a paper card.

15. **A hidden $50 bill**. Mine is in my iPhone case. Other options are in the lining of your laptop bag, on your key ring, or inside your shoe (if you do this don't take it out around other people, they won't want it). Hiding one in your wallet is OK, but I've found I need it most on days where I've forgotten my wallet.

16. **Don't carry a branded camera or computer bag.** You might as well put a tag on it that says "Steal Me Please!" The first thing I do with my camera bag is to get the pliers and take the Canon logo off. The same thing can be said of expensive leather bags. In certain parts of the world you are telling people you are great to steal from.

17. **If you aren't, get a friend that's in one of the megamiles programs.** If you travel with them, they can pull you into the good seats or the exit rows. The folks that log millions of miles often get a different line to call at the airline for agents that can do a lot more than the front line service reps that talk to the general public.

18. **Drink lots of water.** You can get dehydrated flying, and drinking a lot of soda is a great way to get fat quickly.

19. **Be nice to the flight attendants.** You'll find no better example of karma at work. There are many times when they can decide to go the extra mile or stick to the book. If you are a jerk, odds are you've never been bumped up from coach to first class.

20. **Bring a two-foot headphone cord.** Your rental car may have a jack, so you can listen to your own music. It's also good to have one if you are presenting and are going to plug into a PA system.

21. **Choose your friends wisely.** I always introduce myself to people on the plane, as it is a great place to network (do you know how expensive it is to advertise in an in-flight magazine? That's because the people on the plane are so cool). But I don't do it until the pilot announces the approach to our destination. That way if someone sitting next to you is crazy, you only have to talk to him or her for 10 minutes or so.

22. **If you are going straight to business, check your teeth and breath before you begin your final descent.**

More bonus tips from my million-mile traveling friend Chip Griffin:

1. eBooks weigh nothing. Paper books and magazines get heavy quick (don't be afraid to tear out interesting magazine articles and recycle the rest).

2. Don't be bashful about asking the gate agent for a better seat (nicely).

3. When your flight is canceled, go to the club or call the 800 number (as long as it isn't crappy weather over a large area) to re-book (not the gate line).

4. Check the monitor to see when the inbound equipment is expected to arrive to know if you are really going to be delayed (or ask the gate agent nicely).

5. If your flight is canceled and you don't think you'll get out that day, move quickly to get a hotel room before everyone else realizes they need one too.

6. If you travel a lot at the last minute, consider sticking with one hotel chain (some guarantee rooms to regular clients).

7. Make friends with bartenders in cities you visit regularly as they often have great connections/info.

8. Have the hotel concierge give you recommendations. Stay away from chain restaurants and tourist hotspots in your free time and explore places the locals like.

9. Sit near the middle of the first class cabin if you care about meal selection (they start at either the front or back and often run out of one choice before they finish).

10. Carry snack bars/nuts/etc. in your bag for unexpected tarmac delays

11. Check the hotel alarm clock to make sure the idiot before you didn't set it for 3 am and then forgot to turn it off when he was done (and housekeeping forgot to clear it, too).

12. If you really, really need to get up at a certain time, use a wake-up call plus that strange alarm clock since neither one can be fully trusted.

13. Use GPS if you are in a city you don't know well. It can be a real timesaver when construction or an accident strikes and you don't know where to go.

14. Use your blog, Twitter, LinkedIn or other tools to get ideas for what to do when you are in a strange new town.

15. Get one of those travel cases with retractable USB/Ethernet/other cables to keep things organized and compact.

16. Board as early as you can to make sure you get overhead bin space.

17. Dress for where you are going, not for where you are coming from.

Blogs, Videos and Podcasts

People are often surprised that as the co-host of a marketing podcast, when I do presentations on marketing tactics, I always say that podcasting is one of the last things you should be doing if you are going to be using these channels for your message. Having been a music fan all of my life, I love producing audio. But you get a greater return on investment from blogging and video, so you should go that route first.

Blogging is where every organization should start when they begin creating their own content. The ability to write effectively is required in all three channels. But once you are done writing the blog post, you can publish immediately and start the conversation (and ultimately start the lead flow).

I'd like to tell you that blogging is easy and everyone can do it, but unfortunately that's not the case. It's easy to start a blog if you don't mind it looking like a Wordpress Standard template, but if you want something that matches your existing corporate website as far as look and feel, you are going to have to secure some IT resources. Once you have decided on how to handle the IT infrastructure, there's also the challenge of coming up with an endless stream of interesting content. Because of the high failure rate and low subscriber and comment numbers for the majority of corporate blogs, I suggest going the free hosted account route and swallow your pride on the fact that it won't look like your corporate website. The key is to find out quickly if you can crack the code to creating engaging content. By going the low IT infrastructure route (basically free), your only risk is the time and effort that goes into generating the content. If you are able to build an active audience, then you can worry about "pimping your blog" to get it to look great and add in features that you don't get with the off-the-shelf free account.

Every company that I have worked with has the same problem with blogging. Usually the people with the most interesting things to talk about are the ones that have no time to blog. They are often the product managers or lead technical people (often the same folks called into the heavy technical sales cycles), and they are usually quite busy trying to hit things like quarterly sales goals.

At the other end of the spectrum are the marketing communications department folk, who view the blog as another place to post the press releases that nobody is paying attention to. If your blog is going to look exactly the same as the news page on your website, you really shouldn't bother.

A solution to this problem is one that you, as a savvy marketer (buying this book and all), should see as an opportunity. A marketing professional with interviewing skills can use a blog as the media outlet that the PR side of the house is always searching for. You can create compelling content in-house through interviews and case studies of the movers and shakers in your organization and the customers that are doing the most interesting work.

Again, don't get bogged down in the technical side of the blog. These are problems that you can throw money at to make it go away. Coming up with fantastic content that attracts followers? You can't just throw money at that. It's your story and you have to figure out how to tell it. Solve that problem and the rest will take care of itself.

The biggest challenge here is trying to get a human voice in the blog. Large corporations and their legal teams have spent the last century eliminating every last risk from corporate speak, creating a language that is of no interest whatsoever to the average reader. Telling compelling stories using humor and emotion is contrary to corporate communications. But it's a battle you are going to have to fight and win if anybody is going to have any interest in your blog.

As you crack through and begin to write about interesting topics, this content can be repurposed on every front. You no longer have to worry about coming up with some kind of newsletter – just bundle up the most popular blog posts over the past three months and make a digest for the customers/prospects that haven't figured out what Google Reader is yet. You'll find that the mass market sits over on the email side and that your content can have a second shot at life through the newsletter. Note that you should only include a headline of the content in the email that links to the "article" on the blog. This way you can see what content drives traffic from your mailing list.

By starting with a blog, you'll also be creating search engine bait that you would not get if you put the same content out via podcast or video. Every topic you write about is another possibility for inbound traffic. In turn, you can use this to determine what topics will do the most for your inbound marketing efforts. By using keyword generator tools you can look at the most popular blog posts you've done, make a list of the keywords you've covered, and then create a list of new keywords to focus on. As time goes on and the content piles up, this traffic will feed off itself and gain momentum.

Video always has significant buzz as most companies that are working to drive traffic on the Internet are staking their future on the web overtaking television as the channel of choice. As a result, there are always tales about video getting preferential treatment on search engine results, and the siren song of the viral video calls to anyone that dares pick up the camera.

Just as with the blog, the greatest challenge will be keeping the corporate-speak out of the content. You can see the roadside littered with videos that started with a funny idea and then the product was layered on top of that. Unsurprisingly, the laughs usually get squished out by these committees.

The degree of difficulty is high for video. Anyone can write a script, but now you have to catch the magic on a camera, and oh by the way, you better have great sound because nothing can kill a video faster than not being able to hear what's going on. Once you've captured it all, there's the challenge of using a video editing program to cut it down to a manageable length (probably less than 2 minutes) and wading through a murky swamp of file formats, codecs and hosting options.

Like most of the channels that have become democratized through technology, you'll find it's really easy to create a video that has decent production values and sits on YouTube with 12 views and goes no place.

If you still have the burning desire to get your story on video, give it a shot if you have the time to spare. There are many great resources out there you can read, but there's no substitute for jumping in and creating your own. You can get an HD video camera for under $200 and iMovie comes with everything else you need to give it a shot. After that, you are only limited by your imagination and talent. For more on this channel check out Steve Garfield's "Get Seen."

Podcasts are the channel that I have had the most fun with, and that's because anyone involved in this space loves producing audio. But as Christopher S. Penn points out: "You could see that podcasting would not be a profitable channel when the porn and gambling industries didn't jump in at the start."

The problem with podcasts is that with the exception of commuters, there are not a lot of people listening to audio as recreation compared to the number of people that watch video. And for those who do, the allure of professionally produced audiobooks and repurposing of audio content broadcasted over the air, such as National Public Radio, leaves a pretty narrow niche for the independent podcast producer.

Not only is there the challenge of a small audience, but the fact that the communication is asynchronous. With both blogs and video there is the ability to comment and forward the content along as it is being consumed. With a podcast, listeners are often behind the wheel, or on the treadmill at the gym and have no ability to forward or follow a link. One of the reasons for the success of the *Marketing Over Coffee* podcast is that listeners know that if they've heard something on the show that they want to look into, they know that there will be comprehensive show notes with links at the site.

Just as with video, there are some arcane arts and technology to master. You can spend a lifetime learning about how to get the best sound recorded with your gear, and then you'll need to know about file formats and RSS feeds to get the audio up on the web and into the iTunes directory, so that it can be automatically downloaded to your listeners' audio devices.

While the list of podcast millionaires is astoundingly short, the platform can be leveraged to gather a following and drive traffic to other products or services. Sponsors for *Marketing Over Coffee* that sell enterprise software have found that their investment in sponsorship has paid for itself more than one hundredfold over time. Although the audience is small, you do have their full attention. If you manage to keep it, you will never have a better opportunity to not only get your message out there, but also have people pay attention to it.

If you are interested in learning more about podcasting I recommend Libsyn, who I've used for hosting for more than 6 years. They have everything a podcaster needs to get started, including setting up mobile Apps so you can get on both the Apple and Android platforms.

Webinars

"(The) mind, stretched to a new idea, never goes back to its original dimensions."
- Oliver Wendell Holmes

Webinars and online meetings have grown considerably over the past 10 years, and with good reason. I'm amazed that the business travel industry has managed to survive after the one-two punch of 9/11 and the creation of services like GoToMeeting, WebEx, and Glance. Producing a webinar that generates decent leads is not only an excellent marketing program; it's the creation of unique content. It allows you to interact with the attendees in a less-threatening manner than an on-site visit. It's educational and provides value to both the attendees and the presenters.

As with any other marketing program, it's all about the content - The more compelling the story, the better the response. There's also a unique feeling around these web events. On one hand, it's like producing theater: you are creating a live event that is dependent on all kinds of logistics and technology. Everything from the speaker getting confused on time zones to the local power company inadvertently cutting the fiber optic cable to your office can ruin your show. Yet the thrill of producing a great show is tremendously satisfying.

On the other hand, once you finish stressing out over it (I never eat lunch before my 2 p.m. webinars, I just don't have the stomach for it), you'll realize that you can't fail. In the worst scorched-earth scenario, your speaker thinks they go on two hours after start time, and your office Internet and phone connections have failed (all disasters I've run across). You merely send out an email explaining there was a total disaster beyond your control and that you'll be rescheduling and that everyone will get a link to the recording in case the new date/time is not feasible. The key is you have the list! You know who is interested in the topic and that was the goal of the event in the first place, to find out who in your house list is investigating the topic and passing that list on to sales. In fact, you don't even have to tell the world it was a total failure. You could say that "some attendees had problems logging in," because face it, people are only interested in their experience. It doesn't matter if everyone or only they couldn't get in, the damage has been done. I've also found that trying to spin things never works out in our new connected reality, the complete truth is only a tweet away. The old corporate communications policy of never admitting failure just inspires the scorn of the public for presuming that they are not smart enough to Google what's going on.

Worst case scenario aside, there are plenty of tactics you can use to make a great webinar beyond just making sure you have a great presenter. If possible, I always recommend doing your due diligence on presenters. Just because someone has a position of power or influence, and has done hundreds of presentations before, that doesn't mean that when you get them on the phone line that they aren't going to be putting people to sleep. The thing to remember is that this is not the same as public speaking. For the most part, the attendees will not see the speaker. So they need to be able to tell a compelling story on voice alone.

Some simple rules for great webinars:

1. Have a fantastic presenter.
2. Dead air is a killer.
3. Do not let the clock guide you.
4. Have at least two people on the line, a moderator and a subject matter expert.
5. Never open the phone lines for questions.
6. Decide if you want to record beforehand or do a "Live" show.
7. Follow up rapidly.
8. Post the recording.
9. Re-purpose the content.

Fantastic Presenter. I'm beating on a dead horse here, but it's worth doing. If you have someone great doing the show, everything else is just details that can make it a little better or make no difference. No list of tips is going to make a terrible presenter worth sitting through.

Dead Air is a Killer. You never want silence on the line. Because attendees can't see the speaker, you need to keep them visually interested. This is not just about keeping it interesting either. Remember that people learn through three of their senses– hearing (auditory learners), seeing (visual), and doing (kinesthetic). The degree to which teaching toward a single sense works is dependent upon the learner. While some prefer visual and cannot process auditory information at all, others may prefer auditory or kinesthetic. By presenting your material in both an auditory and visual fashion you increase the probability that your content (which, if you've done your job well, is linked to your message and the value you provide to your customers) will stick. As I stop to beat a different dead horse, make sure that your slides are visually interesting and tell your story. Nothing says "unprepared" as well as a slide deck that's made up of the speaker's notes on a bunch of bulleted lists.

Do not let the clock guide you. A common mistake is saying, "This presentation will be 30 minutes (or 45 or one hour, whatever)." If the session is going well, keep it going. If it's limping along, put the horse out of its misery and you can beat it later. A common format is to have a presentation and then open the session up for Q&A. When the questions fade out, pull the plug. One tip here though, just as in live presentations, it often takes a while for the audience to warm up to asking questions. I always keep a few "softball" questions so that when the Q&A begins you aren't sitting there with dead air. After you've done a presentation four or five times, you will probably know what the most common questions are and you can roll those to the presenter right off the bat. Often you'll find that as soon as one or two are answered they start rolling in from the attendees. I've had great webinars that were only 15 minutes and sessions that go a full hour and a half. The thing to remember is that the best-case scenario is to cut it short so that everyone wants to learn more, which can happen in a one-on-one discussion that's tailored to what their specific challenges are. As soon as even a single attendee thinks they've heard everything there is to hear, you are now losing opportunities for real discussions. It's far better to end early than late.

Have two people on the line, a moderator and a subject matter expert. Unless your speaker is exceptional hearing a single voice on the line, this will eventually cause a listener to tune out. By having someone who handles the administrative details (i.e., how to ask questions, introduce the subject matter expert) and a second voice as presenter, you can make the audio landscape more interesting. Having a male and female voice can push this even further. Remember that the key is that they sound different. If two voices sound alike on the line, that can cause confusion.

Don't Open the Line for Questions. This is a common rookie mistake. Just because your meeting software has the functionality to unmute attendees to allow them to ask questions that doesn't mean you should. If you are doing some kind of demo for a small group and you know all of the attendees, then yes, feel free to open the lines so they can ask questions. If you don't know everyone on the line, you can't be sure of what they are going to say when they get the floor. I've seen more than one vendor ask "innocent" questions about who the product integrates with to give themselves some press or exposure to your attendee list. Unfortunately, there's also the fact that as you reach a certain size of attendees, you can always count on a small percentage of attendees being all-out weirdoes that are killing time at work, have no intention of ever buying, and are more than happy to ask all kinds of weird tin-foil hat questions about situations that are possible but never happen in the real world.

Decide if you want to record the session in advance or go live. There are plenty of opinions about the "right" answer to this question, with valid arguments on both sides. Some say that webinars should be live performances and that they are like theater such that each one is a unique performance that's adapted to the audience that shows up. I agree with this. If a webinar is entertaining and answers all of the specific attendee questions, it's hard to get a more valuable presentation. The question here is: Does that extra boost of doing the live tailored show offset the risk if something goes wrong and the event doesn't go off at all? The proponents of recording in advance say that this is a point of professionalism, by having a strong recording that's as close as you are going to get to ensuring that the attendees will not have their time wasted by a failed presentation. There's also more quality control. I'd like to say that every webinar I've done included a complete review of the presentation beforehand, but schedules based in reality and juggling multiple campaigns don't always allow for as much preparation as would be prudent. I can buy this argument too. I've found that a hybrid approach works well — regardless of whether it's recorded or not — I always try to have a live Q&A session. I think there's a lot of value to having interested prospects be able to have their specific concerns addressed. If I have never seen the presenter do a webinar before, it's a good idea to record the presentation and then you can still go live if you want, but at least you have the recording as back up. If I know the presenter is going to show up with their "A-Game" then I'm not afraid to go live without a net. This is also a bit more efficient. Instead of watching it during the first recording and then recording it a second time to get the Q&A, you only have to sit through it once.

Follow up rapidly. As with any prospects, your goal is to get them to the sales team as fast as possible. Leads are not like wine or cheese; they rarely improve with age. One mark of a quality webinar is when you have so many incoming questions that you are unable to answer them all in the session and these unanswered questions get passed on to your sales reps for follow up. Instead of having to cold call, they can dial to answer pending questions. The only leads better than those are the folks asking for pricing or where to send their purchase order.

Post the recording. Even if there are no pending questions you still have a decent list of prospects to engage. After you have uploaded the attendee list you've got the list of no-shows. Depending on the content, you can expect that list to be 50 percent to 70 percent of the registrants. The goal here is to get the recording edited and posted to the web as soon as possible, giving your reps a reason to get in touch, to pass on the link to this content. You may have some resistance about putting valuable sessions out on the web. But the capacity to spread your message rapidly outweighs the risk of your competition getting their hands on it. In our connected age, they've already seen it. If they really wanted it, they can get a common customer or prospect to log on for them and snag it with $30 worth of screen capture software.

Repurpose the content. Many content providers fall short here. Once a webinar is in the can, that doesn't have to be the end of life for it. The recording can be plugged in blog posts or via email. It can be transcribed to be the basis for a white paper, promotional offer, case study, or testimonial for other projects. If the presentation is particularly engaging, it can be saved as an audio or video podcast. Keep this in mind when creating the content. If you are talking about things that are not in the news (that will be out of date in a year or less), such as best practices, go out of your way to make the content evergreen by not mentioning the date or current events. It's not unheard of for webinar recordings to have more than four years of life in them. That's a fantastic return on investment for the cost of going through production once.

The Logistics of a Successful Webinar

The first challenge is getting a topic and presenter. One best practice here is to schedule a rehearsal or recording session prior to doing any promotion for the event. That way if you realize that the topic or the presenter is not going to get the job done, you won't be stuck trying to figure out how to get lipstick on the pig.

If it's your first time using the conferencing service, you need to test everything prior to promotion also. If you send out a round of email and then realize that your vendor is not going to cut it, it's a ton of work to contact the registrants to get the updated login information. Prior to using the service you'll want to test both the audio quality and the screen sharing functionality.

Audio quality. One problem with hosting webinars is that you are going to have to use service providers for the screen sharing and the audio. Like it or not, the performance of these service providers is going to reflect on you. If attendees are not able to log in to the meeting or are watching and the audio quality is terrible, they consider that your problem and if it gets messed up, your brand looks bad. Not being able to login is most commonly a firewall problem for the attendee. The good news is that if this is an issue, odds are the attendee's IT team is familiar how to get around it, or at least you can tell the attendee that their company policy forbids access, so that you don't look incompetent.

On the audio front you will have to do some testing and make a decision regarding cost/quality. There are three types of audio that are commonly used for webinars. Your provider may offer any combination of the three, and may also allow you to use any of the three you already have. Until about three years ago I would only use POTS, erring on the side of high quality. Since then, the integrated dial-up service that GoToWebinar offers has proven to be an acceptable level of quality at an exceptional price. Here's a breakdown on the three sound formats:

1. Web based audio. The audio file is transferred via the web to the attendee's machines. This is quite similar to the service that Skype offers, although many online event providers are not at a comparable level of quality. The benefit of this format is that it's free, and many international attendees prefer this method. The downside is that the quality can be poor, or to make up for quality issues there may be up to a 5 second delay in the audio. Presenters should never use this audio format. Quality is acceptable, at best, and if one presenter is using web based while the others are on phone lines, you'll get an echo or feedback because of the delay.

2. IP based phones. Some conference services offer these, as well as many of the low-cost conference call vendors. This format allows you to dial in on any phone, but at some point, the signal is sent through the Internet. By getting off traditional phone networks this method is much cheaper but may also suffer on sound quality.

3. POTS (Plain Old Telephone Service). The most expensive method and the best quality.

Screen Sharing. At the basic level, most services allow you to show what you have on your screen to everyone in attendance. From there you can add all kinds of features depending on the vendor and on what you are trying to accomplish. It's quite common to require passing the presentation "baton" from one presenter to another – for example, a senior executive introduces the company and big concepts, and then a technical person takes over to give a product demo (although I've found that in those situations you can save yourself the headache of making sure the baton gets passed by having the senior executive send their slides to the technical person so that you can eliminate the handoff).

Another common feature here is the ability to show recordings as if they were live presentations. Most of these tools will allow you to open up a video file and play it, but not all have the ability to make it look as if it's a live presentation. If your vendor has support for multiple monitors you can fake it with some practice.

How to make a recorded presentation look "Live"

If your vendor supports multiple monitors and allows you to choose the one that is displayed, you can keep the webinar console on one monitor and run the recording on the other. The key is to start the video on your second screen, switch it to full-screen mode so that the controls are not visible, and then activate the screen sharing (and know how long the video is so that you can stop screen sharing before you reach the end of the recording). In terms of creating a recording I've not been able to find anything that can beat Camtasia for screen capturing and creating a WMV file.

Another challenge here is getting the audio to the phone line. There are two ways to do this – ghetto style is to have speakers on the PC and have it in a room with a high-quality speakerphone, such as a Polycom. This is acceptable, but you have to make sure that you will not be disturbed.

If you'd like to save yourself a lot of headaches, for about $100 you can get an audio tap that will allow you to run the audio out of the headphone jack on your computer directly into the handset of your phone: http://www.jkaudio.com/voice-path.htm

This will run the signal straight into the phone so not only will there be no quality issues, but it also acts like a mute button. While the computer is providing the audio the handset is rendered ineffective. You can make all the noise you want in the room while the recording is playing and attendees won't be able to hear you. Another benefit of this device is that when you are not playing audio, you can use it to record the audio of the call (for when you are making the recording that you'll be playing later).

Two other "gotchas" to test for – make sure that the default settings for your webinars keep all attendees muted on the phones and unable to see the attendee list. The last thing you want is 40 people trying to figure out what's going on with the phone line noise or to have a competitor login and be able to get a screenshot of all the people you've worked so hard to get to attend.

After you have done your own test run of all the components, you can do your first rehearsal/recording. One tip here—have the cellphone numbers of all presenters and involved parties. If they will be dialing in on their office phones, you are going to need an alternate number to contact them on just in case there are problems. You'll also want to confirm with all presenters the day before that you are getting them on the line for any rehearsals and for the presentation itself. Don't make the mistake of finding out you have a time-zone issues when you and 200 attendees are waiting for a presenter to show up who thinks they are starting an hour later.

During the rehearsal and reminders be sure all presenters understand that they need to dial in, not use the Internet audio. They should also be using a headset instead of a speakerphone. The rehearsal is also a good time to line up "softball" questions that you'll use to prime the queue. Another wild card to address is screen resolution. Technical people tend to have their monitors turned way up, so that everything may look tiny on the most common resolution settings. Non-technical people may also do the opposite, have the resolution turned down so low that everything is easy to see. But it ends up looking like some kind of preschool computer with huge buttons on the technical person's screen. The most important thing here is to decide what resolution you want to record at and make sure that everyone is at that same resolution, otherwise you are going to have a real tough time resizing the sections that are too large or small. And even if you are strong enough with video editing software to do this, it will still look weird, as icons get larger and smaller as the presentation goes on.

You'll also want to go over how questions will be presented and answered during the session. One tip here: You may have to take screenshots of your monitor so you can instruct other presenters how to access the question list. Most screen sharing systems do not show the screen sharing controls (which include the question panel), so it can be challenging to train someone how to use these controls. This will depend on your level of familiarity with the topic. If you know the topic well, it's easy to determine which questions are appropriate and you may not even need the presenters to see the question list. On the other end of the spectrum, if you know nothing about the topic, you will need the presenters to see and rank them in terms of which are good questions to ask, which could be skipped, and which should not be asked (Vendors of Product X tend to show up asking how well your product works with Product X to try to get a free ride off of your audience and hard work).

Once you know that your content is strong, it's time to promote the event. Get the word out there and see what kind of registrants you start getting. One key to better attendance is to review the emails to see who clicked through to read the email but did not convert. Odds are these people are interested to some degree and may only have a scheduling problem for the day of the event. Making a personal call to invite them to the session, and offering them a link to the recording afterward if they can't make it is a great reason for a salesperson to make a call to the lead.

Showtime

"There's no business that's not show business."
- Advice painted on the wall at Jordan's Furniture, Natick, MA

You'll want to log in at least 30 minutes prior to the start. Odds are you won't need this time. However, you'll want to plan on being able to reboot your machine twice if you have any problems and time to contact the online meeting system's support line if anything strange is going on.

Once you start, welcome the attendees to the event and remind them that everyone on the call is muted to ensure the highest quality audio. Tell them that if they are using the web based audio and should they notice quality problems, then they are better off dialing in, if feasible. Inform them on the procedure to questions during the session then tell them the overall agenda.

I've often found it useful to conduct a poll at this point (if your webinar system supports polling). It gets the attendees engaged. It also can give you some insight and gives late attendees a few more minutes to log in before they start missing the main event.

When you are ready to go, introduce the presenters and hand them the baton so they can show their screens. If you are running a recording, you can set it up here, hit play and then relax. I've also found it useful to have a second machine logged in so you can see what the webinar looks like to the attendees at all times. It helps you determine if there's any delay in showing screens, or if one of the presenters is not doing something properly.

After the content is completed the speaker will give you a cue that they are ready for Q&A to begin. At this point you can thank the speakers, answer any administrative questions (nearly every webinar will have questions about where to get the slides and if a recording will be available). This is a good time to run another poll, start with the softball questions and then work into the list.

From there, you can wrap up as your timetable allows. Some will stay to the bitter end to answer every question, others like to wrap up according to the schedule they set, or as soon as a certain percentage bails out. This is more a matter of preference, but I've found it's good to have some of the salespeople in the room. They can tell you if the people asking questions are worth staying on the line for.

Wrap Up and Salesforce.com

There are a lot of opportunities to gather data and connect with prospects after the event. Having this data saved into your CRM system can make this much easier and faster. In SalesForce.com you are able to set up campaigns (groups of leads and contacts organized by the marketing programs they have participated in such as trade shows, webinars, or downloading white papers). As a lead or contact is added to a campaign you can also record a "Campaign Status" such as "Attended", "No Show", "Requested Demo", or "Requested Pricing". I've also found it very effective to add a custom text field called "Campaign Comments" so you can add notes. For trade show attendees you can then include comments like "stopped by booth to meet Dave and requested latest documentation" to make it easier for your sales reps to follow up after the event.

Set up a campaign in SalesForce.com for each webinar and load up the preregistration list with the registered and the leads that clicked through on the email but did not register (campaign member statuses can be set to "Clicked" and "Registered"). You can now run reports on the clickers so the reps can see what their story is, if they can get them to go to the webinar, or if they have any other things they want to learn about.

Another incredibly powerful tool is the exit poll. GoToWebinar has a function that has an exit poll pop up on the attendee's screen when the session is closed. This has proven itself to be much more effective than calling or emailing a follow up survey after the event.

Key topics to ask are: Were they satisfied with the presenter and the content? Did they have any technical issues with the call or the meeting software? Do they have any follow up questions? Most importantly: Would they like to be contacted by a representative?

After the event, you can load this data straight into your campaign. Clickers will remain as such unless they are converted to registrants. Registrants will become either "attendees" or "no shows." Based on the exit poll, some attendees will be reclassified as "Wants Call" or perhaps "Wants Demo." Again, this will allow you to create custom reports for each SalesForce.com user for follow up.

In the campaign member comments you can add any questions they asked during the session and any information gleaned from polls you have run or from the exit survey. Once you have a better feel for the information, you can also use the poll to ask questions that can be loaded straight into SalesForce.com fields so that you are enriching your data every time you run an event.

Posting the recording is another event for you to leverage. You can email all of the registrants that it is available. Also post it on your blog and website if you want the traffic. At this point, you'll have to decide if you want to keep it behind a registration wall. This decision will be driven by how much you want leads. If your sales guys already have 1,000 leads they haven't had the time to get to, you will want to filter out the tire kickers with a registration form. If people are fighting over the 2 names that come in a day, you may want to leave it wide open to generate some buzz and allow you to offer other events and materials.

Another thing to think about is where the content sits in the buying cycle. If it's a basic presentation about who you are or what your product does, you probably want to leave it wide open to make it as easy as possible for large numbers of people to access. The idea is that every basic demo that gets downloaded and watched is one less set of phone calls and introductory demo that the sales team has to do (odds are for the twelve-thousandth time).

If the content is very valuable, involves pricing, or could easily be taken by competitors and used to their advantage, these are situations where you might want to control access. An easy way to get the best of both worlds is to offer a short white paper explaining it in more general terms. Then have links in it to allow them to get access to the deeper contact (allowing it both the spread with no friction and still allowing you to evaluate the ones that are "real.")

After you have a few under your belt, you can start to apply more strategy to creating your content. Odds are you'll have varying results with the first few, but eventually you'll get a feel for what works, and more importantly, what you can use as "evergreen content" to be replayed frequently. From then, that material can be incorporated requiring almost no labor on your part, besides running the recording and tallying the results.

Website Analytics

Website analytics is a field of study that needs to be at the center of the new marketer's skill set and I am quite surprised to find little being done in this area by many professionals. It seems that even after over 10 years of evolution in this field, the majority of small-to-medium sized businesses tend not to go much deeper than the volume of traffic they have coming in. This is unfortunate for a number of reasons, but is also understandable. There is both hard science and a bit of voodoo being used here.

To get to the source of the problem, you have to dig into the technology. In its purest sense you are keeping track of how hard the servers you have connected to the Internet are working. This is critical in order to maintain your little patch of the Internet. If things get too busy your site will slow down, and may even go offline altogether. With the transition to cloud computing, it's common for these duties to be passed up to the service provider, and for many people, this is a good idea.

If you have just joined a marketing organization and have to find out what's going on with the website, it's a good idea to learn what's happening with the server itself. This would consist of checking, at least on a daily basis, the amount of data it is pushing out so you can see exactly what's going on. One area of this reporting that is often overlooked is the amount of data being pushed out relating to images on your website. Because most website analytics packages are only interested in page views, they tend to ignore the volume of data that graphics are generating. This can cost you money in the long run for two reasons. One is that good web designers will optimize the images on the website specifically for Internet use. Designers that don't know what they are doing will often upload whatever they have, which in some cases may be print ready artwork which greatly increases the file size yet providing no visible difference in what they look like. Showing images on the screen does not require the level of detail that printing on paper requires. If your costs are going up based on the amount of data you are pushing, one step is to audit the graphics on the site. Another item that does not show up in page view analytics is "deep linking" of graphics. This is when another website uses the graphics on your server for display on theirs. For example, if someone was on an online forum and was talking about a beer can, and you had a beer can image on your site, the person writing the post could copy the web address specifically of that image and use it in their post on some other website. This is normally not a big deal, until you have an image of someone famous or other newsworthy item. You can end up providing the bandwidth for someone else's images. The solution is simple enough though. Check your server stats to see if you have any of these images draining your server. If you are charitable, send an email to the Webmaster of the other site requesting they remove it. In the event you are ignored, you can use the time-honored Webmaster tradition of changing the name of the image on your site so that it still displays there. Then delete the original image from your site and either put up a 1 pixel image and give it the original name so that's all they see, or if you are a vengeful person, you can get a particularly hideous pornographic image and give that the original name. Suddenly you'll find the offending Webmaster cleaning things up in short order.

Beyond the basics of knowing what's going on with your servers (either under your control or in the cloud), there's the next level of web analytics that attempts to provide actionable information about what people are doing when they visit your website. Because of the nature of how the Internet works, at this point it stops being an exact science. The reasons why are technical and rather boring. The short version is because of the way data is served up, there are many times you are not sure exactly who is getting it or what they are using it for. Many times you can see what appear to be spikes in traffic only to determine that a single user made thousands of calls to your server because of a virus, software failure, or because they hate your guts. My prescription here is two-fold: first you should read everything you can from Avinash Kaushik. He has devoted years to writing up what you need to know in this area. The other is that Google Analytics is a good place to get started given the price point (free). In fact, it's my opinion that unless you have a web analytics system that is giving you a value add of some kind (such as tying into your CRM system), it's hard to come up with a case for paying for one.

Just in case you are not able to run out right now and get Avinash's books, I can give you some general advice that I use. There are thousands of metrics you can track, but the truth is that the majority of them are not going to change what you do on a daily basis. As a result, I spend more time digging into relatively few metrics than watching huge dashboards of data. A wise man, whose name I can't recall, once said "Dashboards! A great way to make it simple and easy to let people ignore data."

Nearly every company I've seen has some kind of web form up as a cornerstone of lead generation. Keeping track of the number coming in on a regular basis, where they came from, and how good they are is a task that means more than 75 percent of the crappy reports most web analytics tools provide. Unique visitors on a monthly basis corrected for seasonal variance is a good board meeting level stat just to get a feel if things are moving up or down. This could be a completely garbage statistic that has no relation to sales, but I still think it's worth tracking for the feel of things.

There is a revolution going on here thanks to the number of tools that integrate into web analytics suites. While the traffic itself is interesting, it is far more useful and relevant to the bottom line to integrate with your Google AdWords campaigns to see how effective your campaigns are, or integrate with your CRM system to see which of your leads were banging around on the site this week. Rather than knowing which pages are most popular, it's far more useful to tie this information to the lead record to be able to say that after a lead registered for an event they viewed these pages. From here you may be able to derive some insight as to what problems they are trying to solve. The problem is that most people begin digging into web analytics by learning about what kind of tools they can play with and what reports can be run. This is backward. The key is to come up with a set of questions you want answered and then determine those tools that will get you to those answers. Even if you know nothing about these tools, you are better off going in with questions about what you are trying to accomplish, rather than inviting all the vendors to give their dog and pony show, showing off reports and features that you will never use.

The questions that concern you might be ones like these:

- When an offer is made on the website, what kinds of results (leads) does it generate?
- When do people tend to give up and leave?
- What are the top ten search phrases people enter in our search box? Could these be eliminated by having links on the home page to these high demand resources?
- What third party sites are sending traffic to our site and is this traffic any good? If it is, is there a way to get more of it?
- How is Google treating us and do we need to do any work in matching the language of our site with what people are looking for?

Another area here that's often ignored is user interface, (UI to those in the know) and the related field of User Experience (UX). There's a whole body of knowledge out there on how to make sure that your site is not sabotaging itself by making information difficult to get to. Jared Spool and Jakob Nielsen are two authorities in this space to pay attention to. But even if you don't have the money to have a consultant help you with skilled design and things like eye tracking cameras to see where users' eyes go when the page comes up, you can still get a ton of value by doing your own low-budget site evaluation.

The key is to create a list of the four or five most common things you think a user is going to want to do on your site. You then pay some students or get some friends and family of employees that know nothing about what you do and have them come in for a user session. Set up a video camera on the screen and then read them a prepared script (same for all subjects) that gives a short overview of what kind of user they are, and what they should try to accomplish. For example:

"You are a person who is looking to buy our product, the AX-15. What would you do when you come to our website?"

"You are having a problem with the AX-15 you own. What do you think you should do when you are on this page?"

"You want to search for the technical specifications for the AX-20. What would you do to search for it?"

You'll be amazed how navigation that seemed intuitive at design time is invisible to the user. Users being unable to find menu options they want, figure out where the search box is, taking minutes to accomplish goals that you would want to happen in less than 10 seconds, all these things are common symptoms that come to light during basic usability analysis.

Web Analytics ties in here too, as you can create a hypothesis on what is holding back your conversion rates, make changes to the site, and then check your results. Note that Google Analytics includes A/B testing so that you can set up multiple versions of pages and have Google serve them up and monitor the results.

This is a challenging and exciting field. Have fun shooting at the moving targets!

Where to Apply the Marketing

Classic marketing has relied on the tired pillars of the 5 Ps - The Product, Messing with the Price, running Promotions, Place (how the product is distributed), and appealing to People.

I learned the Ps at college just like everyone else and thought the model worked until the year 2000 when Sergio Zyman kicked me out of my chair and gave me a double barrel taste of how he does business. The new marketer is not walking around with 5 tools in their little box; they are focused on making things happen in the real world. As a new marketer your goal in life is to realize the five Ms.

Sell more product, to more people, for more money, more often, more efficiently. How do you do that? You throw everything you can at it, including the kitchen sink and toilet for good measure. One important point here is that getting more people is only one of the 5 Ms. Getting the attention of new customers is an expensive proposition. The reality is that in most cases it's cheaper, easier, and faster to get more money out of your existing customers than it is to find new ones. If you already have a relationship with a customer to whom you are providing value, then they are probably willing to believe you when you go to them and say that you have something new to check out. This is an efficient way to do things, compared with calling people you don't know and having them say: "Who are you and why are you bothering me? Where did you get my name from?"

The first step in developing your strategy to use marketing to grow the business is to map out the customer life cycle. You want to create the story of your customer with as much detail as possible. It will start with a person somewhere in the world that has a problem to be solved, how they will find out about you, and once they do, why they decide to do business with you versus anybody else around who does the same thing. It will also include what the evaluation and buying process will be like, how long it will take, what resources they will need to make the decision, what will they experience when they become a new customer, and how they will be trained and communicated with. Many marketers end here, and let's face it, that's more work than the average 6-year-old in a sweatshop is doing. Just as in most things in life, there's not a lot of traffic in going the extra mile, but that's where the glory is. What will the customer experience in Year 2? Year 5? Why would they go somewhere else? How could we win them back? Is it even worth it to win them back? When we have a new product or offering how will we tell them about it? Will they get a discount as an existing customer? This is where the add-ons and upsells live, and this is where you can have a huge impact on your profitability. There's nowhere cheaper to buy new business than here.

Another step here is to document every detail you can about your customers. This practice of creating "personas" has been popular of late and works well to create a common language within the organization. When everyone is on the same page about how "Betty" buys and uses the product, it makes it simple for everyone to talk about what Betty is looking for in her purchase today as compared to last year, and why something that works for Betty may not work for Mary, and so on.

As this map begins to mirror reality the communication points with the customer will be in focus. Odds are you will have your contact points with the customer charted and can then use this to build campaigns, not around your calendar, but around the customer life cycle. Instead of providing value for 6 months, you'll be optimizing your entire business for as long as your doors are open. The email tracks discussed in the earlier section can come into play here. By creating a standard communications plan for customers during the first weeks, month or maybe even a year, you can ensure that their experience is all that it should be without a lot of manual labor.

Once you have the framework built, you'll want to revisit and review the customer life cycle based on the rate of churn in your industry. If you are in an established market, you may be able to get by with overhauling everything annually or maybe even every 2 or 3 years. Regardless of your market, technology is moving so quickly that if you go beyond 3 years, you may be missing new technologies that could be leveraged for profit.

As your system proves itself, you will then steer more resources in the direction of new customer acquisition. Lead generation becomes a major portion of your efforts. We've covered a number of these tactics in the previous section. Each of these tactics will be matched to channels your personas have an affinity for, and this will rank the tactics in terms of which will have the highest rate of return.

Lead Generation

In marketing lore, it's commonly stated that a new prospect will have to see your name eight times or so before they recognize who you are. It may take a dozen or more before they come to mind when considering purchasing a solution to their problem. All lead generation activity is designed to create these 12 touches to get to the top of their mind, and make it happen as fast and as cheaply as possible. The end result is to have successfully introduced your company and product to the lead and pass the information off to your sales team to enter the next stage of the customer life cycle.

Search Engine Marketing

Website analytics often drives search engine optimization (SEO), the art and science of getting the search engines to recognize your website as an authority (and more importantly, send the traffic that flows through the engines to you). This is always the first place to start with your website marketing because this activity has the highest return on investment. By simply cleaning up the code on your website and making sure that you are using the terms that people are searching for (as opposed to the classic old school marketing practice of making up your own terms and market definitions), you will increase your inbound traffic. For a small business starting out, the difference between 2 and 4 leads a week can make a huge difference in getting to profitability. Most of this is old news. I feel ancient telling stories about having done this before the turn of the century, trying to get Yahoo to pay more attention to the database events I was promoting at the time.

The latest step in the evolution of this process is the transition to real time. David Meerman Scott has written about this in his book *Newsjacking*, but to give you the thumbnail sketch, search engine traffic is up for grabs every day. Any time a topic trends upward, it's a chance to generate some inbound traffic. By maintaining an active blog as part of your website presence you are able to capture and ride the trends of the day (or the hour!) to drive traffic.

Eventually, you will have your content building engine scaled up and you will reach a point in which it's easier to buy traffic than to create more content to get it. Note that this is not true at first. In the beginning, you will be writing about your product and/or service and you will have to dominate on these keywords. At some point, though, you will start to move to related topics and you will not be able to dominate as easily here. At this point, the cost of buying clicks from the search engines or social media sites will have a higher return than hiring another carbon-based life form that requires healthcare coverage to write and research.

For example, you may dominate in your category of software development tools and do well there. You know that a portion of your customer base uses the tool for database development, but unfortunately there's a lot more competition both on the SEO and pay per click front (PPC), and unless you think you can go toe-to-toe with Oracle, you are going to have to get creative.

In theory, as a smaller organization you should have no hope. Your competition has more inbound traffic, more resources to buy traffic, and more marketing resources overall, so there should be no opportunity. One of the greatest joys of marketing is that it is both art and science, so it's not just a matter of pouring money in and getting business out. A more creative marketer really can do more with less. There's also the fact that as an organization gets larger, the number of dopey mid-level executives that think they can do marketing increases drastically, as does the number of dopey mid-level executives that demand approval and refusal rights of projects to go along with the status reports and other CYA foolishness that abounds in large bureaucracies. As a result, it's a never-ending battle. The big guys can do a lot, but the smaller guys will be nimbler, faster and more creative, even if they do have to figure out how to do it with duct tape and chicken wire.

The concept behind pay-per-click (PPC) advertising is simple. You pay a search engine to show your ad when users search for the keywords or phrases that you have paid for. From there it gets astonishingly complex. To make things even more challenging, what started out in the world of search engines has created a set of concepts that are now used on many other social media sites and forums. Currently, Facebook advertising is at the frontier of these practices. There are many books on PPC advertising, but my own experience is that this space is moving so fast that there's no substitute for starting small and scaling up with each success. The tools and networks change so fast that you are better off checking out forums and blogs, and running your own testing than reading a book with info that's 6 months or more out of date.

Much of PPC advertising is referred to as a "Black Box" problem. There are a lot of levers you can push and pull in your campaign, primarily the copy of the offer, the landing page, and the amount you are willing to bid for keywords. The problem is that the engine that combines these factors and serves them up in the search engine results is not public knowledge. As you tweak the inputs you may or may not see changes, but you'll never be sure exactly what is happening inside the search engine (the Black Box you never get to look inside).

Regardless where you start your PPC efforts there are some basic principles that will keep you out of trouble.

1. **Select the keywords.** There are two tactics here. The first is to have a short list of three to five words that you are targeting. This allows you to start with a small budget and expand as you determine what is successful. There are plenty of tools available to select keywords, and you should be able to determine from your own web analytics what terms bring people to your site. A word of warning though, this is a self-fulfilling prophecy. Obviously the words you are

using are going to bring traffic to your site. The greatest benefit of using keyword tools is to find related terms that you are not using on your website that are getting more search volume than the terminology you are using. This is why PPC keyword tools are often used in SEO activities. Taking time to ensure that the copy on your site is aligned as well as possible with terms more commonly searched for than similar terms that you are currently using is a great way to get more clicks without having to find any budget.

2. **Understand negative keywords and keyphrases.** This is key to starting small and scaling up. Some terms, such as "mortgage" can have a price per click over $40 due to the intense competition for them. By starting with the phrase "second mortgage" you can significantly reduce the competition you face (and the cost per click). If the engine you are buying from supports negative keywords, this is another way to reduce traffic that is not a fit, or undesirable. In short, when you define negative keywords you are saying, "Give me all the results for my keywords, minus any that include this word." For example, if you sell a premium product or service you may want to add "cheap" as a negative keyword to exclude traffic that wouldn't buy from you anyway.

3. **Control your budget.** Systems like Google have plenty of tools to manage your budget to make sure that you don't do something stupid and rack up $10,000 in clicks in a single day. As you start out you may want to have a campaign active for a single day only. Most likely you'll be starting with a small test budget, and depending on how active the keywords you choose are, you may burn through your clicks in a couple of hours or less.

4. **The Offer.** One of the benefits of this type of advertising is that it's easy to test variations on your offer and see which ones work. You can also throttle

these in both directions. If you aren't getting enough, free white papers and videos can bring the numbers. If you have too many to deal with you can offer to sign up for a demo that will bring lower numbers, but more qualified leads.

5. **Landing Pages.** This is another area that marketing professionals have written volumes on. The basic rules are: make them as simple and short to fill out as possible, do not just make it a page on your website. You'll see that many landing pages don't site navigation on them (which tends to bleed off traffic, making it more difficult to track). Also, if the network supports it, you'll probably need to put some code on your confirmation page so that the ad network is made aware of successful conversions. Although the click data is useful, only conversion data is going to tell you if the program is worth doing in the long run.

6. **Ad Placement.** There are two things to look for here. One is where it falls on the page. For Google, there are a number of available slots on the right side. Depending on how much you pay and what Google thinks the quality of your offer is, you will go higher or lower on the page. As you have no direct control over where you are going to end up, this is challenging to test, but you may be able to learn if it is worthwhile to do what it takes to get the higher slots, or if just being on the page is good enough for you. The other placement issue is that for most networks your ads are going to show up in one primary property, on the right side of the page in Facebook or on Search Engine Results Pages (SERPs for the followers of search engine trades). Larger networks may allow you to buy placement in other properties, such as Google's content network, which places ads on other, third party websites. Pay close attention here because the quality of your results may vary widely across networks and I've found this to be the fastest way to burn up your budget if you are not careful.

If your programs prove successful, you'll also want to integrate these programs with your CRM system. Being able to load these leads, and details on the programs and offers they accepted, is important information to pass on to the sales representative. As you scale up you will want to automate this as soon as possible to eliminate having to key data or upload spreadsheets of results.

What's Your Cost per Lead

Over the past 20 years return on investment (ROI) has been a measure of successful marketing. Many management teams want to see the ROI of each successful campaign. Seth Godin and many others have argued that this is the "safe" path, and will ultimately lead to your destruction. If you only make the safe choices, somebody that you compete with is going to take a chance, and will eventually send **you** to the unemployment line.

So how do you get around this? It may be impossible if your management team is already expecting ROI on everything you propose, but you need to change the ground rules. View all of your marketing efforts as a whole. Given your entire budget, how many leads do you pull in? How good are they? How many close and for how much?

With metrics like this you can determine a cost per lead, and determine how much revenue each lead generates. Now you know the overall ROI of your marketing programs. You can see how every program performs in both terms of cost and quality. You'll be able to make some informed decisions, such as, perhaps Google clicks are not worth the huge dollars and you don't need to be spending so much there. Is Facebook generated traffic worth the same amount as clicks from Google? Which trade shows are worth going to?

The end result is that if your overall activities are generating a positive ROI, you now have an excuse to do some R&D, and you should refer to it as such. Now you don't have to try to make up numbers about what a YouTube video might do for you, or some other program that you've never tried before. You just say that this is an experiment and it may fail, but we will learn if it's possible for it to generate enough return to add to our marketing mix. The great part is that as soon as you get the data you'll be able to compare it to the rest of your programs.

Mac McIntosh says:

"Marketing is like baseball. Not every swing of the bat is a home run, but if the batter doesn't connect often enough, out he goes. Not every ad or campaign is a success, but overall the marketing efforts have to be helping the company meet or exceed its goals or out it goes.

Honestly, why would a company spend money on something that they don't expect to see some return on? They don't just add salespeople because they think they need a few extra. They don't buy an expensive piece of equipment unless they can justify the increased output, efficiency or savings. Why should marketing be any different?"

As an enterprise is born, marketing exists to serve as lead generator. As the enterprise expands, the earlier sections of the sales cycle can be outsourced to marketing automation. If an organization grows large enough, marketing transitions to branding as a primary focus (over lead generation) if it becomes necessary to influence the public, shareholders, or other groups that are not directly purchasing the product. Different skills and toolsets are used during the evolution.

One to One Marketing

"One on one, I want to play that game tonight."
-Daryl Hall

In the late 90s, when the term "Marketing Automation" started to make its way into common use, there was a lot of discussion about one-to-one marketing. I often considered this the ultimate goal of automation, a unique set of communications for every individual.

As efforts for campaigns moved in this direction, I realized that while it was possible that every time a customer gets service they could have an experience tailored to their history (thanks to the miracle of CRM), the ability to create marketing campaigns that are unique for every individual and always relevant becomes impossible at the scale beyond what a single person can hold in their memory.

David Meerman Scott wrote a blog post about his experience with an email from American Airlines that clarified my thinking here. He was bringing to light the absurdity of them sending him an offer to buy 2,000 more miles to use for a family trip (when he, at the time, had a half million miles in the bank – enough to take them first class anywhere in the world). To solicit some comments he asked, "What can we do about this?" And one of the comments mentioned one-to-one marketing.

This reminded me of the "busy intersection" joke in Kevin Smith's "Chasing Amy" (a scene that's offensive and totally not safe for work). To spare you the obscenity of the street joke, if you think you can pull one-to-one off, you probably are also waiting for it to get delivered to you by Santa Claus and the Easter Bunny on their day off.

At the core is a popular buzzword—segmentation. The theory is that if you segment the audience, you'll eventually deliver a uniquely tailored message to everyone. The problem is:

1. Your audience can be segmented infinite ways.
2. Every time you cut a segment you increase the complexity of your system exponentially.

Most marketing departments struggle to get out single messages, so it's near impossible to generate enough content to support all the possibilities in 10 segments (just trying to send two relevant messages to 10 segments could give 100 possible message combinations).

If you really want to get granular – i.e., not just "Is David in the 100k+ group – Yes/No," but instead "Less than 20k in the past year gets A, 20k-100k gets B, 100k+ gets C," the math starts to get ugly real fast – like one of those tables showing how fast bacteria grows.

If you are a hardcore database marketer, you may still be saying, "No problem, I've got the server space to track 20 variables on all 6 billion earthlings," and you'd be right. But here's the big kicker: That only works for one campaign. Let that marinate for a minute. Fast forward six months – Campaign 2 kicks off, even in our nursery school scenario of 10 segments getting two messages, who is going to make sure that nobody gets the same message the second time around (now that you have 1,000 possible message combinations)? Although only linear, that number will still hit the millions in no time.

Regardless of the scary math, it's irrelevant, because even with tiny numbers a year's worth of campaigns are too complex for the human mind to work through, and even if you had a team of "Rainmen" that could, eventually, someone will quit and be replaced with someone who doesn't know the whole history.

So what can be done? Two things. You can use your CRM system to track your customer's entire history. But the important thing is not to chase a marketing fantasy but to use it so that **sales** can create a one-to-one experience. You can also have a list of customer traits short enough for the human mind to comprehend (Are they in the 100k club? Have they been an angry customer in the past year? Are they influential in winning us more customers?) and then tag your customers accordingly.

Repeat, similar, and irrelevant offers are impossible to stamp out just because of volume. There are infinite variations in the situation as well as the criteria (which may or may not be rational) used to determine what data points to segment on. For everyone with 500 thousand miles in the bank, there's one corner case of the guy about to fly all his buddies to SXSW for free and he's only 1,200 miles short, and yet he is so psyched he got the same email that the other huge mile holders considered to be a waste of time (improbable yes, definitely not impossible).

Ultimately you have to ask: Are we more concerned about a small group that may be offended for whatever reason, or the group that accepts the offer? (Hint: One group generates revenue, the other includes some legitimate complainers, people with lots of cats, senior citizens with nothing to do, and people wearing the John J. Wall Signature tin foil hat to protect them from the Government's mind-control rays).

Don't waste your time fighting it. Reap the reward from the happy customers who take you up on your great offer and apologize with a tip of the tin foil hat to anyone you happen to offend.

Lead Scoring

The goal of marketing programs is to match the needs of a lead with the solutions you provide. In a new organization as soon as a lead identifies that they are willing to talk to you, odds are you will be passing it over to a sales person for an exploratory discussion. As the organization grows, the sales function tends to evolve in two ways: first, everyone becomes more adept at communicating what your solution does, and second, you improve in your quest to find a small number of questions that will identify if what the lead needs matches the solutions you can provide. At the start of your business, you will spend a lot of time having these discussions, and probably adapting your product or solution to confirm that you have found your market.

Ultimately, you will settle on what you believe the most profitable market is, and at that point, you will begin working more on sorting out the leads that are not a match. If you've set up the business model correctly, you will have focused your product or service so that it solves a specific problem that enough of the world has so that your business will be profitable. At this point, your marketing and sales cycle switches from aligning the customer's problem with your solution to farming and harvesting matches between problem and solution.

To scale your business for increased profitability, you will shift the screening and alignment functions from sales over to marketing. Instead of sales qualifying every lead that is interested in a discussion, you will create marketing programs that will allow these leads to self identify what their issues and concerns are, which will then allow you to qualify them and determine ones that are a potential fit as a customer.

For example, once your sales team has reached a point where it can close new business, you will examine the initial discussions it has had with prospects. Let's say that one of the first questions is, "Do you use system X, Y, or Z?" The sales team knows that it has a number of customers on system Y, so if there is a match, it will have some ready references and perhaps a 50/50 chance of closing a deal if it can get the lead engaged in a demo. Often sales will also know things like, "If they are on system Z, I might as well thank them for their time and forget about it because that means they are too cheap to buy what we sell" and perhaps "System X is a mixed bag for us."

With this scenario, you now have an idea how to structure your marketing programs and lead scoring. Most new organizations fail here by doing white papers, webinars and case studies along the lines of "Check out our awesome market leading, scalable, flexible solution!" and unsurprisingly, nobody cares about your lead generation program with the same marketing jargon that you are using in your press releases. The lead scoring system in our example would be in this order: Y, X, Z. You know that the sales guys want all the Y leads you can get, X leads are riskier, and Zs are ones you want to filter out. If possible, set up your system so that they never see or deal with them.

Your first round of programs would focus on gathering Y leads. The secret to success here is to focus on the pain that the lead has. Using a basic hook, such as "Best Practices in Using System Y in Your Business" or "How to Avoid the Top 5 Pitfalls of System Y" are short, compelling tabloid magazine style headlines that will attract attention.

Consider what this does: If you were to start with the "Hey, check out our cool stuff" hook, you would then have to determine if they have a problem that you can solve, if they are on the right system, confirm they really do have pain, and odds are sales would be doing the digging here. By starting with a program that qualifies them as System Y users, you skip a number of steps in the process and go straight to discussion about, "So which of the five system Y pitfalls we discussed are you facing? Yes, we have a number of customers that have seen significant success in solving those problems, so significant that our product tends to pay for itself in less than 3 months…"

As your programs get more effective, the goal is to reach a point where you have enough qualified leads for sales that they are doing no cold calling or initial screening. All of these functions have been pushed down to the marketing department so that they scale faster and become more profitable (and one of the true tragedies of business is that marketing people tend to be cheaper than sales people).

If you are fortunate enough to unlock the code of qualifying leads, your problem will be that sales will have too many leads to follow up on. At this point, you repeat the process–determine what the next level of qualification will be and create programs at this second level. For example, after successful screening of System Y, you may find out that if they have System Y and less then 3 people on their team, odds are they are in significantly more pain and now it's an easier sell because it's cheaper to buy your product than to add another employee. At this point, you switch from individual "campaigns" to establishing a relationship with the lead (previously territory reserved only for the sales function). As with any relationship, there will be a number of interactions of increasing commitment. A common progression is "Check out this free white paper, no sign up, no risk, no sales calls," then "Watch our free webinar," up to "Let us give you a custom demo" and so on until it becomes obvious that buying your product will make their life significantly better (or even better, less painful). With every contact point with a lead there is both the opportunity to provide them with something of value to prove that you are going to solve their problems, and the ability to learn something about them that will tell you if they are a good fit or not. In this case, we want to learn team size, so we run our webinar on System Y, which will educate the lead, but at the same time, as we are waiting for attendees to show up at the beginning, or as you are waiting for questions to come in during Q&A, you can throw a poll question out there asking how big their team is, and now you know which leads are in the 3 or less category.

If you're lucky, you'll reach a point of irony where sales will be enjoying the fruit of your labor as leads get more and more qualified until you have automated all but the final qualifying question: "Would you like to buy?" Sales will love these "bluebirds" (leads that show up with a check or signed purchase order), but this tends not to last. Eventually someone will catch on and set up an order page on your website so leads can go straight from programs to closed deals without having to pay commissions. Of course, this depends upon the complexity of your product. There are many things that cannot be sold without some individual attention (and these are the markets that salespeople who are interested in job security focus on).

It should be obvious that for this process to work there needs to be complete understanding on both the marketing and sales side of how the sales and marketing processes work and where the transition is from one to the other. Also note, as both marketing programs and sales techniques become more effective, the transition point will shift to later in the sales cycle. Unfortunately, the opposite can be true also. Some marketing programs will become less effective over time and will either not deliver the same volume, or the market will change in such a way that it will require sales getting involved earlier to determine the quality of the lead.

To determine the exact point that a lead should be transitioned to sales often involves a lead scoring system. At one end of the spectrum there are business-to-business (B2B) vendors that are happy to sell you a solution with a 1- to 2,000-point scale, with every marketing touch accumulating a number of points. You can dial in the transition to sales at X points. This sounds (and actually is) impressive, but I've noticed with more than a bit of cynicism that the complexity is in direct proportion to the cost of the system that does the lead scoring.

Lead scoring will fall into one of two categories. You will either have a solid understanding of the sales process and there will be clear milestones that indicate the probability of a purchase, or the sales process will not be clearly defined and you will use lead scoring to measure activity levels.

Milestones tend to be the classic sales qualifiers: inbound call for information, marketing program activity, discussion with sales, confirmation of budget, negotiation, closed deal. If the sales cycle is well defined, you will add marketing program milestones to the list and you will simply have to select at which milestone the lead will be passed to sales. In these situations the lead scoring system can be extremely simple. A proven scale that I've used before has four possible scores: A, B, C, and D.

D leads are garbage, having confirmed that the contact info as no longer valid, or that they are a category that has proven itself never to become a customer, and therefore is a waste of sales resources. Although a common impulse is to delete the D leads on a regular basis, whether it is to make space in the CRM system, or just the understandable urge to "clean up," don't miss the considerable value in maintaining this list so that you can exclude these names from your campaigns to both reduce cost for campaigns such as direct mail, and to increase the performance and reputation of your emailing campaigns (the higher your open and click ratios, the less likely you are to be grouped with spammier characters). The D list is also a great way to determine the quality of other new lists as you acquire or test them. If you get a new list and you notice a large number of hits on your D list this is a great indicator of quality.

The C list is the entry point into the marketing system. You probably know little about them and the only contact with them would be through marketing programs until they have demonstrated that they have an interest or a need. This tends to be the "holding tank" where the majority of leads in the system will be.

B leads define the transition point. These are leads that through some interaction have proven that there is a need for more discussion. This is the point where the sales rep would do their "cold calling" (of course, the level of evolution of your marketing programs will determine the degree of "cold"). An important point to understand with B leads is that they overlap both sales activity and marketing programs. These leads may be contacted by sales reps, but they will still be receiving marketing communications and promotions as you continue to learn more about the types of challenges they face (indicating their need for solutions and probability of becoming a customer).

The end goal for the lead scoring process is the A lead, which indicates a successful transition to sales. The primary characteristic of an A lead is that the sales rep has taken responsibility for the lead and upon transition of being scored an A lead it will be removed from all marketing communication. This allows the sales rep to take control of the relationship without concern of any special pricing promotions or other communications that comprise the ultimate sin of marketing programs, screwing up a deal a sales rep is actively engaged in. This is the worst mistake on two fronts. It indicates that you do not understand the sales cycle, which clearly defines when broadcast offers are appropriate, and worse yet, screwing with a sales person whose salary is directly related to how many deals they can close will, at the very least, make them want to immediately stab you in the heart with whatever they have lying around the office at the time.

By tracking the counts of leads at each of the four scoring levels you create a static snapshot of the quality of your lead database. As you focus on your sales process, the important measures will be of the rate of change as leads move through the scoring system. These statistics will do an excellent job of showing the effectiveness of moving leads through the system. However, remember that all of these numbers are trumped by only one that matters, the number of them that turn into sales opportunities that the sales reps put into their forecast.

Once a sales rep indicates that they will fully engage with a lead, marketing scores this as a victory. Anything that moves to the A category is a win—**provided that you have mapped your sales process correctly**. The proof of this lies in the number of A leads that mature into closed deals. This is where the structure of Salesforce.com meshes nicely with an effective workflow. Setting up the A category of leads gives you a clear indicator of what the sales team is working on for prospecting, and when they reach a point where they forecast a deal (creating an opportunity in salesforce.com) the lead is then converted to a new SF record called a Contact, which is attached to a record set up for the entire account. This now creates three easy-to-measure milestones for marketing programs: number of A leads created, number of leads converted to contacts, and finally, the only stat that really matters—number of opportunities.

Once the opportunity is created, this is the last point where you can make general statements about lead quality. With the sales rep fully engaged, your results are now affected by the rep's ability to sell. You may be fortunate enough to have a system where sales is a repeatable process and you have predictable results (a world I have never seen). More likely, you will have a full range of reps that run the gamut of not being able to successfully submit a signed contract to reps who could sell a burning man a can of gasoline.

Regardless, every opportunity should be evaluated as part of mapping out the sales cycle. By this point, you are clearly in the sales cycle so there are a number of canned reports that focus on these milestones. Opportunity amount, win ratio, days to close, and competitors faced are all basic numbers that provide you with key statistics about the last mile of the sales cycle. These measures of quality allow you to review the quality of the leads and determine where milestones should be.

In many cases, there will be areas that you are unable to set milestones for, but you do realize that you have a large number of leads that need to be categorized to meet sales' ability to work them. These gaps are most often fixed with activity analysis. My evidence is only anecdotal, but in every situation I've seen, if you have two leads that look the same but one has made more web visits or attended more webinars (more activity of any kind), they tend to be better quality leads. And even if they are not better quality at a certain point, they always prove themselves easier to have further interaction with, making it faster (read as "cheaper") to qualify, which then allows you to move through more of them in a shorter amount of time (read as "more profitable").

This is the type of granular activity scoring that you'll see in many marketing automation systems. A lead gets 10 points for downloading a white paper, 1 point for visiting the website, 50 points for requesting a demo, etc., etc., ad infinitum. A good way to set this up is that whenever certain point thresholds are met, the leads are transitioned to a new milestone (i.e. – 100 points makes it a B lead, 200 points and sales gets an alert and is asked to decide if it should be an A lead). By using these "test transition" email alerts to sales, you will eventually gather enough data to see the milestones and eliminate the activity scoring, or prove that there is no milestone, and activity scoring is the only way to prioritize until a milestone is realized.

Lead Scoring

Many CRM and marketing automation systems include lead scoring. By providing a point value to a lead based on the lead's behavior, salespeople are able to filter a large list so that they only work on qualified leads rather than cold calling.

For the most part, scoring is based on hitting milestones: Did the customer hit this page? One point. Did the person download a demo? Add 5 points. Did he or she fill out the request for pricing? 10 more points. Simple enough. Here are some important things to include in your scoring system:

Lead scores should automatically depreciate. If a lead becomes inactive, its score should be reduced over time until it eventually reaches zero. A lead who asked for pricing six months ago is not as hot as the one who asked this morning.

Set ceilings for score categories. If they hit two key pages, you want the 2 points, but if for some reason (such as passing a link on to the rest of their team), they hit the same pages 40 times, you don't want them getting 80 points. A good system should have the ability to set thresholds.

Alerts beat reporting. Having a report with the score is good, but sending an email or SMS to a salesperson is better. Depending on your product, leads may get cold in a week.

WARNING! Do not give anyone outside of yourself the ability to change the scoring system or to reset the score for individual leads. If people are asking for the ability to change the scoring, it's because the scoring is not working accurately. A score that's higher than it should be is only a symptom; the disease is a fault in the scoring system. As you start the system up, you will have to meet with the sales team on a regular basis to review the results of the scoring system to determine what works and what doesn't.

Handoff from Marketing to Sales (SF Tactics)

As part of the lead scoring system you will have a team made up of members of your sales and marketing team that will be examining the process as it runs. They'll be determining which programs deliver the most qualified leads, at which points the transitions should happen, and then finally when the name gets converted from a lead to a contact.

This creates the two most important milestones to gauge your marketing effectiveness— the point at which leads are converted to contacts and the number of opportunities created from those converted leads. A critical point here is that once the opportunity has been created, this is the last time you can measure the quality of your marketing programs without taking into account the ability of the sales person that created it. If both the sales and marketing teams have agreed to the criteria for converting leads and creating opportunities, you will have some decent numbers in a short period of time (in contrast to the entire deal cycle), indicating which programs create the most leads and opportunities. Unfortunately, there's usually a much longer wait to see when and how these opportunities close. This is where businesses can be made or broken, depending on how these cards are played. Sometimes there is rhyme or reason to it, but other times not. I've seen many variations play out and the problem is that unless you have many large programs, each generating a large number of conversions and opportunities, you'll have a hard time generating enough data to reliably predict future successes.

In the SalesForce.com environment this is a clear milestone. A person exists in the system as a lead until it is converted to a contact. The critical difference is that a contact is related to an account. For example "Joe Davis" can exist as a lead and his company can be listed as "XYZ Corp" but this company name is just a single field in his record. When he is converted to a contact, he will have his own record, but the system will have him listed as a record related to the "XYZ Corp," which has its own record. If Joe is the first record from that account, the account record must be created before Joe can be assigned to that account. The important distinction is that while Joe exists as his lead, you could search for his company name and find him, and perhaps other leads from the same company, but they exist independently. When he is attached to an account, you can then look up the account instead of just the individual Contact records. In other words, while Joe is a lead you can see what the history of Joe's interactions has been. When Joe becomes a contact of XYZ Corp, you can look at the XYZ Corp. and get a rolled up list of all the interactions with Joe, and all the other contacts from the account. This is invaluable during a complex sale in which you need to know what's going on with Joe, Joe's boss Suzy (who will be the one signing the contract), and perhaps Oscar, their in-house attorney (who will be doing everything possible to slow down the deal).

During the conversion from lead to contact, the converter has the option to create an opportunity—to say we are expecting a deal of a specific size, for a specific product and set a percentage of probability. This is the core of the sales team's forecasting ability. When a possible deal hits this point, it's in the pipeline and the organization starts watching it to determine when and if the cash will come in.

It's common for a lead to be converted to a contact without an opportunity being created, especially if the lead is at an account that's an existing customer, or at an account that has a number of engaged contacts already there. On the other hand, if an opportunity is being created, you will always want the related lead to be converted for deal control.

A prime example of a program being impossible to measure in the short term was podcast sponsorship. For *Marketing Over Coffee* we had a number of sponsors that tried sponsoring the program for one or two quarters and had no real results. At the other extreme, the sponsor that stuck with it for more than two years had an astonishing rate of return, a greater than 50x return on investment. Although the sponsorship sent very few leads compared to average marketing programs, in the long run it proved to be more qualified than any other inbound leads. They played their cards well and won big, but I would not have blamed them if they had bailed out after three quarters of having only limited results.

This is why senior marketing positions in many organizations have a frighteningly low retention rate. Team leaders come in, place their bets, and then things play out for the good or the bad and quarterly results are the measuring stick. Few organizations have the ability to take a 3- to 5-year view of their marketing programs, especially when the street demands quarterly success.

Like everything else in marketing, regardless of the unpredictable nature, you'll still want to measure the conversions and new opportunities. Although you may never be completely certain of the results, the programs that generate the most leads will at least keep the sales team busy. This is another recurring theme from this point on – you may never be able to tell which programs are more successful than others. But the failures will be pretty obvious. For example, you may have a hard time judging between the trade show that has a smaller number of leads generated than the white paper, but that created more opportunities (which you can't really gauge until you start to see which ones close). However, when compared to the email campaign for the webinar that had no registrants, you can confidently pull the webinar off the calendar for next quarter's campaigns.

Your goal is to create the workflow for conversions and opportunities. A common hand off is to complete a marketing program by sending out the link to a Salesforce.com report that shows all of the campaign members and their status. These can be listed at different degrees of qualification based on the Marketing Campaign Status Field. For example a trade show list could show "Registrants," "Booth Visitors," "Requested Demo," "No Shows," and other disqualifiers – "Competitors," "Press," "Customer," etc.

As a manager, you'll be able to quickly evaluate the relationship between marketing and sales by watching what happens at this point. In many organizations, the departments and managers play nice. But often campaign results are "thrown over the wall" and at this point marketing feels they've done what they said they were going to do, and don't really care about what the sales guys do with them. On the other side, the sales team has probably had these garbage lists thrown at them before, and may ignore them completely.

More effective marketing organizations will demonstrate their ability to work with sales here. After handing off the list, it's best if the marketing team communicates on a regular basis with the sales team to see how the leads are progressing and if there are any ways to qualify or evaluate the list faster. One helpful field in

Salesforce.com is the "Read by Owner" field, which will show if the lead owner has looked at the record. You'll be able to get an instant evaluation of your leads after a week by looking at how many new leads have been ignored. If everything is being looked at and you are getting solid feedback on which leads are better than others, odds are you'll start to see some conversions and opportunities. If things are not being looked at, you've got some cultural barriers to get over, and perhaps some painful work to do.

If you've never dealt with the painful side before, there are two approaches that are common. One is simpler—going to the management team and getting some top down procedures put in place. Like many simple top-down proclamations, they tend to end up in binders placed on shelves, forgotten as soon as they hit the shelf, then it's back to business as usual. The only tactic that I have seen to be effective is to work one-on-one with the reps to prove success. There are two factors to rate the sales team members by. There will be those who take advantage of programs and those who do their own prospecting, and there will be reps that can sell, and those who are on the list to fire if things get bad. Find reps that you can work with that are successful in both these attributes first. By demonstrating to them that you are not just throwing them names but continuing to work to further qualify the leads, and by continuing to drill to find the two or three characteristics that determine who is ready to buy, you will eventually get them to the point where they will be looking forward to getting the latest list. Yet again, this is as much science as art. Finding the right people to work with is as much personality as hard numbers. In fact, you may want to try taking a risk on a rep with low numbers to see if you can create a turnaround story that could generate more success for you across the board, rather than making an already successful sales rep a little more successful.

This is where your career can be made. You can be a marketing person that throws leads over the wall while sales says that you don't get it, or you can have sales reps that consider you a valuable member of the team who wouldn't want to have to do their own prospecting.

To cover the process:

1. Start by getting names in the door so sales has an alternative to dialing the phone book.
2. Try out a wide variety of programs to get different types of leads in the door.
3. Segment these new leads by how they have engaged in the programs to try to learn which segments are more qualified than others.
4. Get the leads to sales and work with them on a weekly basis or better to get feedback so that future lists can be further segmented or qualified.
5. Review the conversion rates and creation of new opportunities to gauge the success of programs and target the losing programs for elimination.
6. Circle back on programs after the handoff to see which sales reps are following up on the leads. Determine who is on board and who is ignoring the programs then come up with a plan to create champions if necessary.
7. Consider the average time to a closed deal. Schedule programs for review to see which programs actually bring in revenue. This may highlight some new successful programs that generate few leads but have exceptionally high close rates, or some turkeys that generate tons of leads that never result in business (note that these are particularly evil programs because they consume sales cycles).

Repeat until the market is conquered.

Blind Spot Contacts

For the most part this process is straightforward: leads come in, some are converted, and some have opportunities created. Eventually the opportunities will be closed as either a win or a loss. The odds are that the majority of leads will not convert. There is a subset that is created here that, at some point will require analysis: converted leads that end up in limbo. A number of leads will be converted and attached to accounts, but will drop off the radar and never create an opportunity. This becomes a bit of a blind spot because once the lead is converted it will no longer be included in all of the marketing programs set up for leads. It may also be attached to an account that has made a purchase in the past, so it may even look like an existing customer even though this individual has never been through the buying process and may have an unmet need.

Once you have a strong calendar of programs and have a short list of three or four that you can count on to generate business, you will reach a point where you should dig into the blind spot to see if there's any money there. By now you should also be adept at getting data in and out of Salesforce.com. I've found the Excel plug-in for Salesforce.com to be an excellent tool for data exploration. You can start running reports to give you answers to questions such as "Show me all the contacts in accounts that have no opportunities, or no opportunities won." This kind of digging has two probable outcomes: you will find some qualification clues about contacts or accounts that never get to closed deals for some reason, or you will find a group of contacts that are much more qualified than new leads because they have already been through a portion of the sales cycle and are familiar with your solution already—they just haven't been able to buy.

Some Things to Keep in Mind Regarding CRM

It goes without saying that for the price you are paying for your CRM system, you'll want it to house everything, if possible.

Major Categories of Information Include:

1. Basic contact data.
2. Data used to qualify leads.
3. Social network profile information.
4. Data loading tools.
5. Qualification points.

6. Opportunity information.
7. Upsale opportunities.
8. Contracts and other documentation.
9. Post-sale communications.
10. Self-serve support.
11. Problem tracking.
12. Champion tracking.
13. Reference tracking.
14. Loyalty programs.
15. Lost customer tracking.

Like any IT Project rollout, you'll have to decide if you want to take a lot of time and effort to scope out the project, or if you'd rather jump right into it with a short list of the most-needed features and then iterate as you go. Both approaches have merit. If you take a large amount of time with the planning, odds are you are less likely to paint yourself into a corner as you add features and solutions. If you start simple, you get all the benefit of the solution quickly instead of waiting around for the planning group to get things together.

Regardless of your timeframe, you will want to create a team that is responsible for the rollout, adoption, and ongoing use and development of the system. This team must have representation from every department that will be using the system, so that proposed changes can be examined for impact across the organization.

This is also a perfect opportunity to examine your current system to determine what information is required and where improvements can be made. If you are building your new data map based on your previous system or if you are considering adding new fields to your existing system, you'll always want to review fields already in use to make sure that you don't already have the data, or that there isn't a similar field that is not being utilized.

The most important thing to remember when creating the map of data that you will be gathering is that the data itself is of no interest. What's important is solving your organization's problems and increasing efficiency. Unless there is a business motivator behind a piece of data, there's no need to record it. One of the most important duties of your implementation team is to defend against "Wouldn't it be great to add X to Salesforce.com," when management is looking for data for this week's project. Unless there is a long-term factor related to the customer's experience, you don't want to be adding fields that will never have data put in them.

Major categories:

Basic Contact Data is close to complete right out of the box. One common addition is the "Left Company" field. Although this can be set up as a checkbox, I've found it useful to set it up as a text field titled "Active?" with the drop down "Left Company" as an option. Sales reps can easily overlook a checked box, but having "Left Company" clearly written on the record is hard to overlook.

Data used to qualify leads are custom fields that help determine what products the lead is interested in, what needs they have, and perhaps other buying signals such as budget or authority.

Social Network Profile Information as part of your prospecting. You should determine which social networks are most popular with your customer base. From there you can track any relevant networks. Having usernames and hyperlinks to user accounts of leads will make it simpler and more efficient for sales reps to learn about them and will allow you to monitor and continue the conversation in real time with customers.

Data Loading Tools. You may find it advantageous to include fields that will allow you to more efficiently load data. Any time data is bulk loaded into your database you will generate a corresponding amount of manual labor required to ensure that you are not creating duplicates or loading dead records. One field addition is to have the email domain of an account as a field in the account record. This will make it easy to identify leads that are probably matches for existing accounts (and also make it simple to identify the lead owner based on who owns the account). Having unique ID numbers for accounts will allow you to distinguish between similar account names. Also, many data providers will have unique IDs for accounts that you may want to append to your records to make it easier for updating these accounts in future uploads.

Data loading can be labor intensive and you will reach a point where it becomes cheaper to use tools such as RingLead, which will identify possible duplicates as part of the upload cycle. Although you may have the labor on hand to stretch the project out and complete it in 2 months, as opposed to 2 days with an automated solution, remember that there is a time value to getting the correct data into the system. There's usually a benefit to being able to start working leads within a day of them coming in, and any time a match to an existing record is found, duplicate labor is eliminated and you may have a lead that reaches a new qualifying point as opposed to a new cold lead.

Qualification Points are usually saved as fields in an opportunity. These are often the data points the sales team uses to determine the probability of winning the deal. A common breakdown is 25 percent for initial interest, 50 percent for engagement with the sales force, 75 percent for negotiations in progress, and 90 percent for contract in progress. Being able to map open opportunities by probability and expected close date is the heart of the sales forecasting process.

Opportunity Information goes beyond the qualification points and dollar amount. Any checkpoints can be recorded, as well as contact information for key players. It may also be useful to have drop down fields here of competitors and incumbent products so that you can later analyze which deals are more likely to be won or snatched away by competing products. It's also good to identify **upsale opportunities.** Based on this existing deal closing, what will they probably purchase over the next year? Automating follow up for potential upsale simplifies workflow for the sales rep, and is good for the organization as reps are promoted to new territories so that new reps have an existing pipeline to work.

Contracts and other documentation will chew up a lot of storage. But having all of this critical information in the cloud available to all at any time leads to considerable efficiencies. Scans of original contracts, details on pricing, any special considerations or concessions can be kept on record to avoid future misunderstandings.

Post sale-communications. Because this is no longer just Sales Force Automation, you will be tracking all touch points during the customer life cycle. Allowing your customer representatives to have access to the customer's entire history will allow you to provide superior service and hopefully eliminate having to treat every inbound customer call as the first contact with your organization.

Self-Serve Support could have a book of its own. Salesforce.com has a large amount of functionality so that common solutions can be accessed both within the system by support agents, or published on public or customer facing websites so that self-serve is possible. This is one of the high-return applications of technology that increases service, reduces customer downtime, and reduces expenses.

Problem tracking is another key benefit to a CRM system. The ability to flag any contact with a pending issue will allow you to tailor your discussion and activities to resolve customer issues, identify customers in pain as soon as they call in, and over the long term, evaluate and report on what the causes of customer problems are.

The flip side of this functionality is **champion tracking**, having a field to identify the most important customers. The qualifications for being tagged a champion will be unique to every organization, but nearly all organizations have them. Whether it's the customer that brings in 20 percent or more of the company's total revenue, the client that's the CEO's neighbor, customers that are also members of the media or best-selling authors, there are always individuals that are significantly higher risk than the average customer, and it's much better to know that in advance.

If prospects require references before they will make a purchase, **reference tracking** is required functionality. Like other data points, it can be as simple as a checkbox, or as complex as multiple fields tracking any relevant reference data, such as how long it has been since they were a reference. Can they do public speaking? Do they have any special qualifications based on how they use the product? Note that having a field to identify references then lets you use this as a qualifier so that you can search on any other field in the database, including geographic area, opportunity type/size, competitors considered, etc.

Data for **loyalty programs** will be generated from closed opportunities and can start as simple reports and can evolve up towards custom applications if necessary.

Lost customer tracking consists of understanding what the end of the customer life cycle looks like. Reasons why customers leave can be an invaluable source of data when looking at the next iteration of the product, or as a bellwether to see when the competition is advancing. There are many other reasons to track former customers. It's often worthwhile to create communications specifically for this group that already understands your products and may be interested in upgrades or new offerings. It's also critical to match these contact records to incoming new leads from marketing programs so that they are recognized and never treated as new leads.

If you are in the initial phases of a CRM project, hopefully this list will allow you to get a project green lit without having to go through a huge ROI analysis. Although many CRM consultants have made a living off proving the worth of a CRM system, hopefully the points above will help you make the argument that this is not just talking about the profitability of adding one more employee or adding a factory. This is the next step in the evolution of communicating with your customers. Think of it more along the lines of "Was it worth it for businesses to start using the telephone? Or email?" You'll never have to worry about proving the adoption of your CRM system if you have the "Why" of creating it laid out from the beginning: having a single point of reference for all the actionable data on a customer will create a "collective memory" for marketing, sales and customer service that, once in place, no one would imagine trying to work without it.

Action Items and Summary of Key 2

Big Ideas:

1. Tell your story. Appeal to emotion. Overcome the temptation to make something that blends in and attracts no attention.
2. Be remarkable – in your Blog posts, email (relevant and compelling), Webinars, PR efforts, direct mail, and your presence at events.
3. Test, test, test.

Leveraging Technology:

1. Start basic with email marketing and continue to extend all the way out to Taguchi testing.
2. Inbound marketing leads are the best you can get, optimize there first. After that explore pay-per-click.
3. Create content and then repurpose – Create content for a webinar, then use it for blog posts, videos, white papers and for content in email campaigns.

Applying to your CRM System:

1. Gather data to support the sales cycle – discover the points that determine if a prospect is going to buy and track these milestones in the CRM system. The sooner you have this data the sooner you will be able to get an accurate measure of your prospecting and sales pipeline.
2. Lead Scoring – if you are successful in lead generation you will come to the point where you will have to prioritize leads for sales. Even if it is as simple as hot,

warm, and cold, this can have a dramatic impact on the effectiveness of your sales team.

3. Review the quality of leads and the pipeline generated with the sales team. By having reports and dashboards that show incoming leads and pipeline generated on a weekly basis, you'll quickly see what's working and what isn't.

Key Point #3

Education: The Sales Function

"(Trust in a team is) an attitude: doing the most for the team will always bring something good for you. It means believing that everything you deserve will eventually come your way. You won't have to grab for it. You won't have to force it. It will simply catch up to you, drawn along in the jet stream, the forward motion of your hard work."
-Pat Riley

Let me preface this section saying that although I have worked as a sales rep, the purpose of this section is not to teach you how to sell in the classic manner. There's a huge array of materials available on that front from people like Zig Ziglar who have already covered this ground and do it in an educational and entertaining manner. Many would like to believe that new technologies change what sales is, but that's not the case. Technology can turn an industry into self-service, or provide the sales rep with a wide array of tools to better tell their story, but ultimately the sales function remains unchanged—there is no substitute for one person helping another through the decision-making process. Just like marketing creatively, this is all about human behavior and there is as much art as there is science to it. Even questionable tactics, such as high-pressure sales will never go away. Some buyers are basically self serve, while others may need to be "coerced" into a deal even when it is in their best interest.

The goal here is not to discuss the human behavior of selling, which is filled with lessons on rejection, perseverance, coaching and making persuasive arguments, but rather to outline ways to make sure that the sales rep has as many tools as needed to make the persuasive arguments. This is at the center of the common ground that sales and marketing shares—great salespeople tell a compelling story to their prospects and transfer the excitement of the product or service to them. Great marketing people build compelling stories and then work to adapt these stories to every channel available to them. The marketing team fills the sales rep's quiver with arrows for every situation and personality. The sales rep gets to know the prospect and through their expert ability to communicate one-to-one and evaluate the prospect's challenges, is able to select the arrow that the customer will buy to slay their specific dragon.

The End of Cold Calling

"You call that a sales call?"
-Seth Davis

As you can see from the division of labor that I am presenting here, the idea of raising awareness of your product falls upon the marketing department. Educating prospects and navigating them through the process to solve their problems, or giving them access to new opportunities is the heart of the sales cycle. Looking at the process in this manner, we will drive cold calling into extinction (pause for cheers from the sales team). Granted, we will not be able to eliminate the possibility of making phone calls to people you have never met before, but we are at a point where you should never be calling people you know nothing about. At the minimum, marketing should have you prepared with data on two fronts: information about the account (the company or organization the person works for), and some personal information, at the very least, accurate contact info and a rough idea of their responsibility in the organization.

A better marketing organization will provide you with a profile of the account that will tell you where their pain or opportunities are and give you the ability to find similar accounts that are existing customers. This in turn makes it simple for you to talk about how you have found success with similar organizations and provides a clear map to success with them based on what you have achieved with your other customers.

Here teaching comes into play by providing educational tools to give the prospect all the information they need to understand why they should enter into a partnership with you.

Depending on the prospect's level of technical sophistication it may also be possible to have a profile on the individual including everything from professional organizations and publications right down to Facebook profiles containing information on their passions and hobbies. This is the area where integration to social media networks can deliver a payoff. Being able to quickly identify who should get the baseball tickets among deals in progress can transform these programs from boondoggles to effective sales tools. This is also extremely useful in identifying references and product champions without having to do any digging for them. By monitoring what is being said about your product, references will come to you much like inbound marketing leads.

There are two spectrums that will define what the sales cycle will look like. Every product is different and the characteristics of your product and the ability to educate prospects about it will determine how labor-intensive the sales process will be. The first variable is the complexity of the product. The ability to describe the value of the product simply and succinctly is the majority of the challenge here. The faster you can get the idea of the product across to a prospect, the less effort it will take to make the sale. At one spectrum is the toilet plunger—it doesn't even need an elevator pitch. Most prospects arrive at the hardware store with an urgent problem, go to the plumbing section and most can derive the solution and use just by looking at it. At the other end of the spectrum is the "complex sale" which may have two problems—a product that is difficult to use or understand, and worse yet, one in which the prospect does not even realize that a solution to their problem exists (often called a "missionary sale" requiring an "evangelist"). You'll often hear terms like "latent pain" in these types of sales. Prospects are living with problems because they are not aware that there's a better way of doing things.

On the complex side it's common to have two or more sales people involved with a sale, one to do the prospecting and a technical specialist that's called in as the deal reaches a higher stage of qualification.

The other factor that will define the sales cycle is how the prospect goes through the decision making process. In our toilet plunger example we have the salesman's dream— the prospect holding the plunger at the register with a wad of bills in hand, eager to get home to apply the product. Unfortunately, at the complex end of the spectrum, the decision process may also be astonishingly convoluted—selling to a Fortune 500 company where there's a committee that will review the product and competitors, perhaps for months, before making a recommendation to another set of executives (or a committee!). Those executives or committee then determine a final deal and contract (not after some time spent in the legal department combing over terms and conditions!), before the ultimate sign off. Here is the world of the sales rep chowing Tums to deal with the frustration of the complex sale. Of course, this cost gets passed to the organization, while the guy taking the cash for the plunger at the hardware store could be making minimum wage, the circle of professionals doing well selling enterprise solutions to Fortune 500 companies usually have to pay taxes quarterly and are concerned with things like expensive cars, summer homes and boats.

The good news is that although this is a complex two-dimensional model, you only need to concern yourself with the problems in front of you today. For a new business this means getting the first couple of sales closed to generate a handful of happy customers to spread your story. Again, we begin with the three major roles—the person who creates the product, the person that generates awareness, and the person that manages the relationship with the customer. Of course in an entrepreneurial setting, one person can be all three roles, as soon as you can specialize these functions, the faster the business will grow.

At the start, there will be no cold calls, but there still may be very little information about the lead, probably not enough to call them warm, especially in the sales rep's opinion. In the beginning the information may be as sparse as "We know they use this product and we work well with that product" or "They clicked on a link in an email we sent them to read a white paper we offered them." Regardless, this makes finding starting points for conversations considerably easier. Coupling knowledge of their organization with knowledge about the individual adds another level of possible discussion points to establish rapport with the prospect.

Being able to open the flow of communication is the first of three stages to creating a customer relationship. Once the ability to communicate has been established the second stage is educating the prospect about the product so they realize the benefit to them. Answering the WIIFM (What's in it for me?) question is the purpose of the education phase.

To start, this education will all be done in person-to-person discussions. This allows for significant feedback in both directions to understand what the best ways to explain the product are, and to learn what the most common questions or points of misunderstanding are. Eventually you will reach a point in which parts of the education process become rote— sales reps will go on auto-pilot doing demos, phone reps will talk about topics without having to consult scripts. This is not because they are bored, but rather that after presenting many times they will have the timing down perfectly (including knowing which jokes work and when to pause for the laughs), and already know the three most common questions and the answers that work best for them.

By evaluating the sales process on regular intervals, sales and marketing can identify refined processes and bring automation to bear. Instead of every sales rep doing a 15-minute presentation three times a day, you can create a video of the presentation that is now available on demand 24/7. It can be watched, passed along, re-watched, or even scheduled as a webinar or presentation if having a date on a calendar will make a group of prospects more likely to watch it. You have now created a productivity gain by removing work from the sales rep's workflow, and also raised the baseline for qualified leads. Instead of having leads a bit above cold, you now have a few more qualified leads that have interacted with the demo coming in. This process continues to be repeated, and leads can continue to rise in level of qualification before being passed up to an expensive sales rep, and your sales should scale accordingly.

The third and final section of the sales cycle is the negotiation phase. Most of the time this will overlap with the second phase. Prospects will want to get a gauge on pricing as soon as possible; sellers will want an idea of how long it takes things to get approved and if there are any competitors in the picture. At this point, the product has been deemed a viable solution or at the very least, enough to provide some value. Hopefully the solution is not just a negotiation hammer to use against some other vendor they want to use (the infamous "Silver Medal Contest"). This is where the "deal making" takes place. As you evaluate your sales cycle, you will reach a certain point (often around the $10 million to $20 million in sales annually range) at which marketing can provide useful analysis on pricing, success versus competitors, and other statistics that can help you optimize your sales cycle. But for the most part, once the deal is being discussed in earnest, the lead generation process has reached a successful conclusion.

The most important thing to do at this point is to have a follow-up discussion with marketing to examine the lead and find out what made it successful and see if more can be sourced in the same way. There will also be another level of evaluation as time goes by to determine if there is any relationship to the source or characteristics of the lead versus the probability to close, and programs will be adjusted accordingly. Finally, the performance of the reps themselves can be analyzed to see if there are any trends in regards to reps that have unlocked keys to success on their own that could be duplicated across the board.

Having been through every step of the process, all that remains is to continue evaluation on a regular basis to take every opportunity to refine and scale as possible.

Guiding Prospects Through the Library

As the prospect goes through the decision making process, a number of classic sales strategies come into play. It is critical for the sales rep to determine which prospects are serious. Some questions to consider are: Do they have budget? An urgent need? The power to make the decision? At the same time the rep helps the prospect go through the decision making process by helping them evaluate the quality of the match between the problem that they are looking to solve versus the value your product or service provides. A common (and effective) tactic is to go through a dance of reciprocity, with each side giving and taking information and concessions, escalating in size as trust is generated by successful completion of prior rounds. Insert your classic sales analogy of going on a first date before asking for marriage (or even more crude relationship function) here. First-round interactions will include simple email exchanges, white paper offers, free samples, etc. Here is where the best sales reps shine by being able to navigate through these early rounds of interaction and accurately evaluate which prospects will end up as customers and filtering out the rest.

Marketing assists sales by providing a library of content that allows the sales rep to explore the needs and desires of the prospect. In an early stage, interaction marketing can provide sales with a library of introduction letters that can be used to move the prospect through the exploratory process at an accelerated rate. For example, many organizations have a single "boilerplate" introduction email. Prospects that respond to this offer then enter into further discussions. By creating a library of introduction emails that can be used to better classify prospects, you allow the sales rep to skip the first few rounds of exploratory discussions. Company A uses an introduction that says, "If you have problems with X, Y or Z, give us a call to see how we've solved them for P, D, and Q." Company B has three introduction emails, one for each of X, Y and Z. By taking the time to determine which one is appropriate by better profiling leads or creating a multi-touch campaign over time, the leads qualified by this program are further along in the sales cycle than the leads passed by Company A. Again, we have our recurring theme of eliminating the expense of labor in the sales cycle through marketing automation. Leads are better qualified and sales cycles are faster and more predictable.

A common problem in many organizations is the gap between the library resources produced by the marketing organization and what actually gets used during the sales cycle. Thankfully, this is another area in which new technologies make this far easier to measure than in the days of printed brochures. A common source of this problem is that the marketing organization often creates resources from the company's point of view, rather than that of the prospect. There's always a new brochure for new or updated projects, logo changes or new corporate vision statements requiring updates to all materials in the library, and I could go on and on with bureaucratic reasons why marketing materials get created or updated and why sales people ignore them for the most part.

The key is not the pieces of content themselves but the relationship between them. How does a prospect get from one piece of content to another? As a best practice, you would have a complete map of the customer life cycle and have the marketing collateral library as an overlay to show you which resources are in demand at specific points, and more importantly, how a prospect's selection reveals a data point that will predict future behavior for you. When you adopt this approach to creating marketing material, you'll suddenly find everything snapping in sync with the view of the customer. Every piece of material will have a call to action in it that will ask the prospect if they want to learn more, or to evaluate their current situation (and hopefully convince them to take action). By having a line connecting your collateral you will know which pieces are most important and will be used even before you create them.

As you begin, you will rush to create the first line from initial interest to sale. Normally this consists of the prospect asking the following questions: "What will the product/service do for me?" "How much does it cost?" and "Who the hell are you anyway?" The classic corporate response is to view these questions through its own bias of "Who the hell we are is really important" even though the prospect doesn't care at all until their first two questions are answered. Another mistake is to use messages like "Our product has all kinds of cutting-edge features and cool new technology" rather than talking about the product in terms of the value it provides to the prospect. And finally, the classic message: "Let's get to pricing later," which generally means that we make our pricing up based on how much work it will be to sell you and how much we think we can get out of you, a best case leaving you with only a pork barrel to wear after having talked you out of your shirt, tie and pants.

Prior to the Internet, this kind of sales and marketing was effective. Now it's just a waste of time. Not being able to describe your product in terms of value to the customer is simply the result of incompetent marketing. Spending a lot of time establishing how important you are before demonstrating value is showing off baby pictures that nobody is interested in looking at, and anyone can get a rough idea of pricing with a bit of Googling. Worse yet, your competitors are more than willing to make some numbers available on your behalf, and you can safely presume that they'll happen to make themselves look like a much smarter alternative to your product.

As we discussed in the beginning with product marketing, being able to accurately describe the value of your product to your customers is an art. Doing it right is capturing lightning in a bottle, but you have to do it. The good news is that it's an iterative process. Start by taking your best shot and refine, refine, refine. Have your story out there and easy-to-memorize and repeat. Have your pricing available (at least a rough idea) so that your prospects can self select as to whether engaging one of your reps is a waste of time or not. Contrary to popular marketing, who you are is relatively unimportant. Why you do what you do is the most important message you can send, and although you may have to tell this story yourself at the start, your goal is not for you to tell this story but to have your customers telling it in their own words. The faster you create a content library built around customer success stories, the faster your sales will grow.

After getting a first straight line created (i.e. introductory email, first phone call script, product and pricing information, materials required to close a deal) you can then test variations to try and find more efficient methods to communicate. A critical point here is that unless you are dealing with huge volume, it's not worth the effort to test on individual pieces of collateral, but rather test multiple pieces in a complete campaign. Working on variations of a single email may only pay dividends when mailing to hundreds of thousands of prospects. Depending on your scale, it is more worthwhile to test complete paths. Start with a track such as first email to solicit demos, followed by the demo presentation and close with a sales call. Then later you can ask: "Instead of progressing from email, demo to sales cycle, would we be more effective with a telephone call and online survey in that same mix? Does it give you more actionable information? More prospects over all? Or does it hit the threshold of "too much communication" and reduce the response rates on the email or number of demos requested?" Considering alternate paths to qualifying customers allows you to test and retain the focus on the customer lifecycle.

CRM Tactics

To help evaluate the quality of leads and the ability to move prospects toward a sale, you will want to record the position of the lead on this straight-line process. At the very least, you will want to track leads that have engaged to some degree (visited the website or downloaded a resource), those that have engaged sales resources (initial discussion, provided demonstration, requested pricing), and those that are in the pipeline to becoming customers.

This data is your first view into measuring the effectiveness of your marketing programs and your first set of data points in creating a sales pipeline, to ultimately forecasting revenue. By tagging leads it's relatively simple to build a suite of reports showing the number of prospects at each point to create the first funnel. More advanced analysis would include how fast prospects move from point-to-point, attrition rates at each point and mapping this data back to marketing programs to measure the effectiveness of the program and the degree of qualification of prospects that came out of the program.

Audience as Asset

Author Ron Ploof has done a sizable amount of research around the concept of "Audience as Asset," the idea that the size of a devoted audience has a direct impact on the corporate balance sheet. We can take this as fact because we realize that in this new era of communication, the endorsement of an existing customer to a prospect that faces the same problem is worth far more than any testimony provided by a sales rep about the product. Like any asset, your audience will depreciate over time if you don't put in the resources and the effort to maintain it. Customer retention is covered in a later section, but what we are more concerned with here is being able to guide a prospect through the sales cycle by providing as many relevant customer references as possible. In what could be described as "perfect marketing," no work would have to be done—the prospect would hear about your product based on peer references, whether it is over the web or through simple conversation. The prospect would verify what they've heard by using their social network to find other customers and confirm that your product is in fact as good as you say it is. A savvy buyer will have everything in order prior to even contacting you. Google talks about the concept of the "Zero Moment of Truth," the time when a prospective buyer does all their research even before contacting you, and this is similar to the concept of "Inbound Marketing" as advanced by Brian Halligan and Dharmesh Shah of Hubspot. Both these concepts promote a large part of the buying cycle as self-service, with the work being "outsourced" to the prospect at the beginning of the cycle.

Again, the value of designing marketing materials around the customer life cycle shows its value. If your customer life cycle is aligned with the reality of the buyer, the resources that you have created for your sales team should also serve as self-service for the savvy buyer. It's also important to note here that by lowering the barrier to access these materials, you increase the probability that they will spread faster. Links to resources that explain your product are simple to pass along. The possibility of one prospect reading about your product and passing links along to the rest of the team of 20 is far more effective than one sales rep pounding away at the list of 20 hoping she or he can get one to pay attention.

Of course this "content rich" model feeds directly into optimizing your content for search engines. There is a huge list of resources covering these topics if you are into search engine optimization (SEO), and if you are interested in working specifically on it. There's no end to the amount of work and research that you can do on this front, but the truth is that if you just focus on creating great content that's easy to share, you'll see the search engines delivering results regardless of whether you are focusing on them or not.

When leveraging the audience as an asset in the sales cycle there are three types of customer references, each having different value and ability to affect a prospect during the buying cycle. At the low end of the scale is the satisfied customer that works for a small- to medium-sized business. In the consumer space this would be the testimonial of someone unknown. These references are either priceless or worthless. When you are starting out and have no references, they are priceless, as they are the only ones you have. As time goes on and you get more referential customers, these will move close to worthless. The worth of the other two types of references are measured in relation to the prospect they will be presented to. One is the "Similar and Not Famous." If you are selling to Joe's Pizza and have already sold to Bob's Pizza two towns over, this is the kind of reference we are talking about. As far as the United States or the world is concerned, very few people know who runs Bob's Pizza. But you can be sure that the folks at Joe's Pizza are aware of them and can probably make a trip over there for a quick discussion. If your prospect has some familiarity with the reference, the ability for the reference to influence the buying decision is significantly enhanced (and note that this does not ensure success, but rather raises the stakes that the reference alone will kill or make the deal).

At the other end of this spectrum is the "Celebrity Endorsement," in which your reference is a Fortune 500 company or other organization that all of your prospects are familiar with. Although not as powerful as the "Similar and Not Famous," many senior managers are big fans of these because they tend to have influence across the board instead of only during relevant situations. Ultimately, you'll want to test these against each other and there are a huge number of factors that will determine what might work best. Personally I'll take "Similar and Not Famous" over the "Celebrity Endorsement." If your buying cycle is anything more complex than determining what kind of soda you want with your lunch, your buyer will eventually realize that the celebrity does not have the same kind of problems/budget/situation that the prospect is dealing with and the endorsement is not worth that much. It may also become suspicious, especially if you are using it for every deal. You are not going to allow any personal contact with the celebrity to avoid burning them out (every good sales rep has some references he saves for the monster deals). It's a lot more work to manage and maintain a list of "Similar and Not Famous" references, but this is the kind of task tailored to a CRM system.

CRM Considerations for References

Again, remember starting simple and expanding as need grows. At first it's enough to have a check box for "Reference," but as time goes on you'll want to be tracking more information. Eventually, changing this from a check box to include a date field "Reference Since" will help identify long-term customers. From the reference's time in the sales cycle you should already have a wealth of information concerning what systems and solutions they have in use. From there it is easy to run these reports on everyone with the "Reference" box checked to come up with customized lists of references. Then the sales team can match them up with prospects that have as much in common as possible.

Two more areas are worth tracking for references. One is that all reference activity should be recorded in the contact's record—that way it's easy to see when a reference is already engaged in a deal, or when a reference needs some time to actually do their own work instead of selling for you (or perhaps it's time to get them a round of golf, vacation, high tech toy, or whatever to keep them happy). The other is to include the reference on any opportunities that are generated, so it's easy to see which references show up most often on closed deals (or perhaps more important, which references never seem to pan out). Although it's initially more work to gather this detailed information, in what should now be a recurring theme, the more complex the sales cycle the more the value of this information appreciates as time passes.

Creating Ambassadors

Another variable to test during the sales cycle is the impact of face-to-face meetings. Having personal contact between prospects and sales representatives can help or hinder the situation, but it is worth testing. If getting a prospect to a customer event where they can meet their future account representative and talk with existing customers can shorten a sales cycle by a year, suddenly spending a few hundred thousand dollars for an event can have a huge impact on the yearly numbers. A little ingenuity can work wonders in this space too. Consider scheduling around existing industry events to take advantage of large numbers of prospects and customers already being gathered. You also can test personal meetings in the area around your home office to determine what is feasible without generating considerable expense.

If face-to-face meetings are effective, this creates an argument for setting up your sales team with geographic responsibility.

Although it seems counter-intuitive in this age of connectivity for a single representative to be limited to a specific patch of land, it will pay off considerably in running local events. One thing to consider here is having a model that has more than one representative for every territory as resources allow. Unfortunately, the current wave of social media tools allows the local representative to gain a higher profile on their own in a market. Depending on your competitive situation, the stakes have never been higher to hang on to a strong local representative.

As a sales rep learns their territory, they will become experts in identifying the "Similar but Not Famous" references for their market. With every prospect and customer now able to inquire or publish his or her own opinions, to have a strong local presence with an understanding of that market is to drastically increase your ability to understand and capture information about that market.

These ambassadors are the face of your company and your ability to solve your customer's problems will be judged by the prospect's opinion of them. Make sure you are putting your best foot forward.

Optimizing the Sales Cycle

Once you get to the point where you are no longer depending on closing deals to get paychecks to clear, you'll be able to examine your sales cycle to see what you can improve to become more effective selling. The first order of business is to manage the pipeline of deals to get a better idea of what your income flow will be. Even after making 10 sales, you can start to measure things like average time to close, average deal size, and probability of closing. These types of stats are your first step away from sleepless nights hoping deals come in, and your first step toward managing your pipeline so you can hit your numbers to the penny like many of the classic cooked book organizations (I'm not suggesting anything duplicitous or illegal, I'm saying the key to success is effectively managing expectations. OK, maybe that and sandbagging is a good thing).

One problem here is that many organizations waste a lot of time on pipeline analysis. The reality is that there are so many factors between the quality of your sales rep, to the applicability of your product to the market, to how much your prospects are willing to lie during the sales cycle (remember, "Buyers are Liars"), that most analysis ends up creating a lot of graphs and PowerPoint slides, but tend to have no impact on the real world. There are a few trends to examine though.

Sales rep performance across the board. For some unknown reason, sales teams tend to show a normal distribution of performance, a few high achievers that crush it, a few that can't sell anything and a bunch in the middle doing so-so. Although I've never come up with a good explanation for why it always looks like this, I can say with confidence that if your sales organization does not look like this it's either because you have a product problem (in these situations nobody sells anything), or you have a phenomenal product and your salespeople are just order takers regardless of what they are telling you (everybody is making big money). In the no sales scenario, fix the product (yeah, I know, real easy for me to say here in the comfort of the coffee shop); if you are at the "Beanie Baby Frenzy" don't touch anything, just start a second team to work on self service sales. Odds are this will piss off the sales force but there's not much you can do, reminding them that normally they have to work for sales is not the kind of message that goes over well.

Stalling Points. By having the sales cycle points mapped, you can see the number of deals at certain stages and determine the percentage of success at specific points. This will allow you to examine individual rep performance, and let you prioritize which points to work on. You can do a lot of complex formulas to determine where to put effort, but in reality it's not worth much because you can't accurately predict how successful you will be in improving the process. You can mathematically prove that if you increase the conversion rate from point A to point B by 10 percent for $20,000 you get a 400 percent ROI, but you're just placing a chip based on your gut that you are going to get that 10 percent lift. One good rule of thumb is that it's usually a safer bet to optimize as close to the point a deal closes as possible. If you improve a process earlier in the funnel there's still a portion of this increase that will leak back out of the funnel. By working near the bottom of the funnel you have the highest percentage chance of your effort resulting in cash in hand. Another way to apply this rule of thumb is to realize that the closer to the top of the funnel, the more you will be looking for an exponential improvement to have the same impact as a change at the bottom of the funnel. Ultimately it will come down to your gut and your ability to crunch the numbers. For $10,000, would you rather get 5,000 new leads or two more prospects to go from having requested pricing to a closed deal? By understanding the flow of deals through your pipeline and having at least a rough idea of where leads leak out of the funnel, you'll be able to take an educated guess at these kinds of dilemmas.

Dealing with Competition. If you are facing competitors, you should have a pick list in Salesforce.com to identify them as part of every opportunity record. When it comes time to close the loop on how a product is doing, having an accurate picture of when you are beating or losing to the competition is essential. Unfortunately, sales reps spend most of their life being beaten up about what they are going to bring in this quarter, so trying to get competitive information through them tends to be limited and heavily biased against the last month's worth of deals. Being able to quickly generate reports over the past 2 years to show wins and losses versus specific competitors allows you to identify strengths and weaknesses. You can develop additional programs to exploit situations where you are winning, and determine if it's worth the time and effort to go back to the drawing board for situations where you are losing. You'll also want to examine these and take into account the largest deals and the average deal size. You may find markets worth attacking and others that are best left to the competitors so they can burn resources on these less profitable deals.

Unseating Incumbents. Depending on the level of maturity of your market, it may also be useful to track the products your customers are or were using prior to being introduced to your product. From one perspective this is a form of competition. From another it will accurately measure your strength in the market. You may find there are some incumbents that are easily dislodged and others that are not worth the time, as they have a history of never closing. Like competitive information, this data is also useful on the product front. The ability for a product manager to run a report to see which incumbents are targets makes it relatively easy for them to dig in and get more information directly from prospects rather than dealing with anecdotal data from sales.

Ability of Marketing Programs to Accelerate the Flow. One of two fronts where marketing can improve the sales cycle is in moving deals through the pipeline faster. As previously discussed, using self-service, online videos as opposed to cold calling, and trying to schedule demonstrations can squeeze weeks out of a sales process. Normally any sales work that can be automated will tend to accelerate the flow, and there's the added benefit of these resources being available online, able to generate search engine traffic and increase total deal flow. Promotions are also able to accelerate the flow, but these should be used judiciously. The problem here is that given the near perfect flow of information, last quarter's "one-time special pricing" will be considered your new pricing by savvy buyers. There is a school of thought that says promotions of this type are only manipulations, and constitute a "race to the bottom" pricing mindset. For the most part I agree. But in some situations, especially emerging businesses, sometimes making the quarter is a matter of life and death for the organization. Measures that established industries would never consider may have to be used by those fighting for survival.

Ability of Marketing Programs to Increase the Flow. By analyzing the source of opportunities, you can evaluate the ability of marketing programs to generate opportunities. This is not a perfect science, but you can get accurate enough to determine what's working. For example, you'll never really know if the lead that came in from a trade show that resulted in a deal would have come in anyway on their own or from another marketing program, but at least it indicates that the trade show is hunting in the right forest. You will have more certainty about the failures. Looking back on closed deals, it's not uncommon to see that some marketing programs never show up as having generated any of the leads involved in the opportunity or generating opportunities themselves. The ability to drop programs and divert funds to testing new ones or stepping up successful ones is critical to running an effective marketing organization.

Deals that "Never Die". Depending on the complexity of your sales cycle, you may see deals that slide in and out of the pipeline. If the sales cycle takes more than a full quarter, you are going to have situations where prospects have budget when they start looking and then may lose funds as other departments take them or as the forecasts change. You may find that deals that were close to closing and then pushed out may be far easier to close on the second time around. Setting up an automated program to review deals that have fallen off the radar after an additional 6 months or a year can be incredibly effective in leveraging the resources used to train the previous prospect about your product. It's just a matter of the right combination of factors on their side.

Buying Cycle Time. As you begin to acquire more data, you'll also be able to generate some statistics on how often customers buy. In situations where you have lost to competitors, you should be able to diary activities automatically for when the prospect will reach points where they will be either revisiting or renewing their purchase, or when you know the competitor's product will be due for replacement. This is another area where you can create leads for no additional cost that have no learning curve to climb regarding your product. As you take a more strategic point of view, you can plan around this buying cycle and create special offerings for certain types of products, if there are markets that you seek to dominate (targeting a specific competitor for example).

Increasing Deal Size. Metrics surrounding deal size can be extremely valuable. Understanding why certain deals are larger than others can give you insight to divert resources toward larger deals only. If you are fortunate enough to crack this code you may find that there is a price point where you are willing to leave deals to competitors, or have self-service web pricing below a certain point as you know it's not worth expending sales resources to chase these smaller deals. One of the pitfalls of chasing larger deals is trying to avoid the trap of time-to-close increasing exponentially. If the deals get more complex as they get larger, you are not only playing bigger stakes poker, you're playing fewer hands, which may give you a chance to win huge, or start making cash flow a headache. I consider this a lower priority item because you won't have to think about chasing this. Most boards and senior managers are going to force you down this path anyway, and odds are they will be involved with these discussions given the possible impact on finances.

Measuring Price Elasticity. Price elasticity is an economics term that describes the relationship in price versus volume sold. For example, price elasticity would be linear if, for a 20 percent decrease in price you sold 20 percent more product. Price elasticity is rarely linear, but we're not interested in graphing a curve. The important thing is to try to get a rough idea of how pricing affects volume. You could spend years digging into these kinds of formulas, but at the very least you should have an idea of your fixed versus variable costs (what expenses do you still pay if you sell one or a million items, and what expenses are paid per item?). You have to consider pricing from the supply side—what it costs you to make and sell it, and the demand side—what are buyers willing to pay and if it gets cheaper will they buy more. As you gather enough data on closed deals you will have the tools you need to experiment with pricing to see if it's worthwhile.

Close the Feedback Loop with Marketing

Although the majority of this book talks about the data flowing between sales and marketing, this data is worthless if the sales and marketing teams are not reviewing together and sharing candid information about what's working and what needs to be changed.

All of the pipeline management techniques above should be reviewed by sales and marketing on a quarterly basis, if not more frequently. Discussions about successful programs, how to generate more leads, the quality and quantity of leads and what numbers have to be generated to meet the company's financial objectives are all topics that are all open for continuous improvement.

I have purposely avoided the topic of compensation for sales and marketing as this is primarily based on market factors, but there is one strategic point. Normally sales is commission-based to some degree, and there has been a trend of driving marketing in this direction. There have been some studies done recently that show that commission based marketing tends to push your programs toward quarterly targets and this has a tendency for marketing to suffer on an annual or multi-year level. This is critical when you consider that marketing is your source of data for product marketing, and your product life cycle may be years or even decades. A good way to get around this is to compensate marketing on annual financial targets (which can be mapped directly to sales goals), but not to quarterly numbers or specific numbers of deals or leads. It's fine for marketing compensation to be at risk (and I would say it's foolish not to), but letting marketing hold the line to look beyond quarterly numbers is often the only way to ensure growth in the long term.

Transition

The final step in the sales process for most organizations is the transition to customer. When looking at the customer life cycle this is a critical point as the customer is no longer a prospect. Many customers feel abandoned at this point in many organizations as the salesperson moves on to the next deal and the former prospect starts to work with the rest of the organization. There are three simple things that can eliminate most of the problems that arise during this transition.

First is to have a documented procedure for the transition. Identify all of the things that happen as far as paperwork, delivering the product, training, handling payment, etc. The procedure should include how to handle the most common problems that arise during this process

Second is to keep the sales representative involved. It's fine if they tell the new customer that they will not be hearing from them as often, but many transitions are much simpler if the customer has a familiar person to call if trouble arises. Better organizations tend to gravitate towards keeping the sales rep involved at some level because it's far easier to upsell an existing customer than it is to find a new one and start from scratch.

Third is to have regular checkpoints on the customer life cycle timeline. At a bare minimum, checking in with the customer on an annual basis is a minimum of service. This will be determined by your business model and profitability. The higher your margins and price the greater the service you can provide (and probably will be expected of you).

As sales reps build a book of business, eventually you will have to look at their workload. It's unreasonable to expect that they can continue to add customers, provide a consistent level of service and prospect for new business indefinitely. Eventually you will also have to have a transition plan as reps leave or change positions. If your business is more transactional in nature, you may be fortunate enough not to have to do a lot of work on this front. But if you are providing ongoing services, proper account transitions can have a significant impact on profitability.

Action Items and Summary of Key 3

Big Ideas:

1. In this era of self-service via the web you need to put all your customer resources online. Any time a

prospect cannot get access to a resource they need, the sales cycle is slowing down.

2. The more you can educate about your product the faster your sales cycle will be.
3. Create Ambassadors – customers that rave about you are better than any marketing program you can create.

Leveraging Technology:

1. Exterminate the cold call – with all of the online resources available a sales person should have a profile of everyone they call; educational resources can be tailored to every lead.
2. Build a library of content for your sales team. Many of the same resources you use for marketing will be relevant to the sales cycle.
3. Track your ambassadors across all social networking channels.

Applying to your CRM System:

1. Track which materials prospects have used.
2. Examine deals to determine who is buying and why.
3. Clearly define the transition of a lead from marketing to sales and use your CRM system to see the health of your lead generation process and learn how to improve it.

Key Point #4

Customer Retention: Serve to Keep Customers Happy

After the Sale

As a new business starts, there tends to be a lot of discussion with early customers and little needs to be done on the customer satisfaction front. The product marketing team is often working side-by-side with prospective customers during early sales and are acutely aware if the customers are happy or on the rampage.

For some reason, I've seen a cultural change as many companies cross the $5 million in sales mark where the ratio of employees that have direct customer contact tends to shrink significantly and it can be difficult for the organization to keep the needs of the customer at front and center in several aspects. Product marketing, marketing communications and sales will need to set up systems to manage customer feedback, and this information has to be passed on to the rest of the organization.

Although there are an infinite number of ways you can survey customers and you could read from any one of hundreds of books on methodologies and tactics, you can apply the Pareto principle here to get the most effort with the least amount of work. The statistic that has the most bearing on your business is: On a scale of 1 to 5, how likely are you to recommend us to a friend? With "4" being very likely and "5" being absolutely, the percentage of

4s and 5s you get can give you a quick and accurate picture of the level of happiness of your customers. Now you may be fortunate enough to be in an industry you dominate and you could care less about how happy your customers are, but I've never seen a situation where ignoring the customer made anything better, and at the very least you'll notice that your sales cycle can get exceptionally ugly when buyers are being forced to deal with you.

The problem with gathering this information is that every organization knows it's a good idea to do it, but a much smaller number have this as part of the customer life cycle. When you step back, you'll see that this is common with all "Business Vitamins," things that improve the business (especially those that don't have an impact in the immediate quarter) tend to be the first thing to drop off the list when the screws are tightened on everyone to meet the quarterly goals.

A good marketing organization should be doing some kind of surveying on an annual basis at minimum, even if only to gather data for their budget and marketing plan. Something as simple as asking customers and prospects which publications they read and which events they are planning to attend over the next year can provide a ton of evidence for how the marketing budget should be allocated. Not asking for references for possible new customers at least once a year is leaving money on the table.

This does not have to entail a major expense. You can use a tool like SurveyMonkey for far less than what it would cost to take a team of four marketing people to lunch and promote it with an email blast to generate some traffic. Another benefit here is that these services generate conversation, and although all of it might not be good (in fact every survey usually generates at least a small number of painful conversations), at least you will have a more accurate picture of what's going on in the market rather than staying in the ivory tower assuming that everything is fantastic.

The next step beyond doing massive surveys is to incorporate a "drip" program. From the sales cycle you'll have a list of the most important data points for every prospect and you'll want to keep these current for your existing customers too. Every email contact you have with a customer gives you the ability to directly ask them questions that will fill in the gaps in your customer profile. You can even indirectly infer and confirm information – include an article in a customer newsletter on a specific topic like, "How to use our product with Problem X," and then provide a click report to sales or your marketing research team to verify that the interest is there because they use Product X. This kind of derived information may require some labor but it is significantly more effective than cold calling.

Another point to be mindful of is that even once a customer is on board (especially in business-to-business sales) there are many times in which the customer will remain antagonistic to maintain a position for negotiation. For example, if your product is subscription based or has an annual fee, don't be surprised to see a lot of negative customer feedback prior to the renewal. This is also quite common in organizations that have individuals or departments dedicated solely to sourcing. Often these individuals get incentives for driving better deals, so they are willing to do or say anything to save a few dollars on the next transaction. Again, organizations that have a deep understanding of the value their product provides, and perhaps has created benchmarks across a number of customers, will be less likely to take a beating during these types of negotiations. One simple tactic here is that often your product champion will take the role of "good cop" and the purchasing agent that of "bad cop." From a customer intelligence point of view the bad cop is of no value. Get all the information and communicate with the good cop to learn as much as you can. Depending on your understanding of the true value that your customer is realizing, you may also want to take the role of good cop and create your own bad cop who can openly say that you are more than willing to drop them as a customer (and you will probably have no trouble finding someone in your organization that truly feels this way and won't have to do any acting).

Your customer life cycle model will show four primary outcomes from ongoing customer discussion:

1. You keep them as a customer and perhaps even gain additional business.
2. Create a reference for additional business within their organization.
3. Win a reference for other prospect organizations.
4. Move them to a status of former customer.

Although the first three have clear upsell potential, the fourth is also valuable. For a product with a high learning curve, having a champion that moves to a new organization can often result in a quick sale in the current organization. Depending on the reason that the customer has left, they may return to a quality prospect status quickly. If the situation changes and they become a prospect again, they should be the easiest to sell having already been on board.

Understanding the reason for customer loss is another point of great importance and low urgency that gets lost in the quarterly cycle. On the positive side, former customers are great future prospects, so understanding why things have changed can be a source of some of your highest quality leads. On the negative side, the first signs of product problems will be evident here whether you choose to examine this information or ignore it.

Some common pick list items for categorizing former customers:

Customer Finances. If their business model is broken, they may not have the cash flow to buy. In these circumstances, you will want to have updated information on your product champions, as odds are they will be at new organizations in the near future. One variation to explore here is to make sure that the customer is not using this as an excuse, when they are actually defecting to a cheaper customer. This can be problematic to diagnose, as customers that want to avoid confrontation may find it much easier to say, "We don't have the budget right now," than to tell you that they've worked a better deal with your competition. Unfortunately your ability to get to the truth here will depend on the quality of your relationship, and if they are lying to you, your odds are probably not good.

Lost Champion. Regardless of the value you are providing a customer, your champion may be replaced by someone with less foresight or an axe to grind. In these situations you want to find out what's happening with your champion and then work quickly to find/create a new champion. Worst case, you may be categorizing this instead as…

Lost to Competitor. For your largest accounts this should never come as a surprise. At the very least, most organizations will give you some kind of opportunity to let you make a heroic save by making concessions to keep the business. It's not uncommon for this to happen with accounts that you are paying less attention to because they are not as profitable. Depending on your ability to measure the value of the customer life cycle, there may even be a subset of customers where you categorize this as a win. It's quite common to have a large portion of complaints and customer service expense incurred by a relatively small number of customers. It's also common to have many of these at a point where the expense to handle them is more than the revenue generated. What a wonderful gift to be able to gift wrap these customers and let your competitors use their resources on them.

No Longer In Market. This can happen from a shift on your side or the customer's. Perhaps your company has decided to stop selling a product for a certain market segment and determined that it will never be profitable. On the other hand, the customer may make the same decision about staying in the market that you provide products for. In these cases, you will consider your product alignment and track your champions, but it's probably game over.

Product No Longer Needed. This goes straight to your business model and requires examination. If a customer finds it easier or cheaper to say goodbye to you, you need to quickly understand what the problem is with your product.

Raising Champions

Post-sale you can categorize your customers in at least four categories:

1. Champions—Your best references and customers.
2. References—Customers who get a lot of value from your product and are willing to tell others.
3. Customers—Excluded from the upper two categories for specific reasons or because you don't know them well enough.
4. Possible Liabilities—There are a number of reasons customers can fall into this category. In the interest of kindness, let's just say that most people acknowledge that the bottom 10 percent of any field should probably be doing something else for a living. As a result they may be difficult to work with, incompetent or some other reason exists that may make this relationship less profitable (or even a liability).

Most business models can ignore the possible liabilities; simply write them off, as there will never be any upside to this segment. Another mistake many organizations make is setting up all kinds of rules and barriers to deal with this segment, not understanding that rules made to deal with this 10 percent are imposing more work on the other 90 percent of your customers. You need to be smart enough to see the difference here. If you aren't, odds are a competitor of yours will be, and you'll pay the price for that through customer defections.

The customer segment is really a catchall and odds are that you just don't have enough information about them to determine if they are a good reference or even a champion. The majority of your effort should be directed toward building references and champions. Part of what makes champions and references is the ability to sell. They need to have the communication skills to tell others about your product and the value they derive from it (again, a big part of sales being the "Transfer of Enthusiasm"). As you begin to determine and develop your champions, you'll find it much easier to identify people that have this ability to sell and give them what they need to succeed with your product rather than take your most successful customers and try to teach them to sell.

The key to learning who the champions and references are is to make your customer community as active as possible. By having customer discussions and events you can quickly see who the great storytellers, inventors, and true champions are.

User Groups

There is no substitute for getting a group of customers together to meet personally. Travel costs may be prohibitive and it may be painful, but you cannot generate more conversation in a shorter period of time than gathering a group of people. First, you are removing all barriers to communication by making it face-to-face and in real time. The other benefit is one that every sales rep understands—you will never get closer to the truth than in this instance, when the information comes rapidly, and more importantly, you can gather intonation and implied meaning as well as any nonverbal cues that are lost on the telephone or via email.

Yet again, the most common resistance to the user group is the lack of return within 90 days. There's also the problem that you could just as likely finish with a huge list of customer complaints after having them gang up on you rather than it just being one big love fest. The truth is, if there's negative sentiment out there, the sooner you hear it and deal with it, the better. But this tends not to fly in a bureaucratic CYA environment where burying dissenting votes is important to maintaining the status quo.

The bigger question is whether your company's culture can stand letting customers get together to provide feedback. It's quite possible you may answer that "No," and then you should probably ask yourself if you are getting paid enough and having enough fun to justify working in this dysfunctional environment. Otherwise, if you think getting customers together can work, there are some steps you can take to get there.

Like everything else, start small and expand. As part of the product marketing function many organizations work with a customer focus group to gather information. This can be a small group of champions, and if necessary, all within driving distance to keep expenses down.

There are three possible objectives to pursue every time customers get together:

1. Get existing feedback on the current product and how it's being used.
2. Gather feedback on new products or possible new products.
3. Train and educate customers to make them more effective.

One other point that is often overlooked, but Salesforce.com has exploited brilliantly, is that you'll notice that #3 above overlaps with the education required as part of the sales cycle. Once your user groups have progressed to a point where you know you are not going to be ambushed, and better yet, maybe some of your customers are talking in public about how they are looking forward to going to your event, you should consider inviting prospects to these events. Letting your prospects participate in an active community of successful customers and letting them make some new professional contacts with your champions and references can make your events a great source of leads and new deals. There's no better way to sell your product than to sit back and let your successful customers do it for you.

Getting feedback on the existing product and how it is being used is best done in smaller groups. Before you get to the point of having events, you can start by doing one-on-one meetings with customers, then perhaps bringing in smaller groups of 5 to 10 customers at a time. Often, you will already be doing something like this as part of your product marketing function. Do not overlook the opportunity to provide your customers with some opportunities for education and networking. An activity such as a meal or event unrelated to business can go a long way to creating more open communication.

Remember that your customers evaluate the value of your relationship, not just by what your product does, but also by intangible items such as helping their professional development, making their daily job more interesting (or less painful) and providing networking opportunities for their career in the long term. The same applies to you. By building an active, vibrant, and successful community, you will be more successful in the long run, not only with the product you are currently working with, but for your entire career.

Focus Groups

Focus can be considered a subset of user groups—gathering of customers, often for a short period of time, to get specific feedback, often on a product about to go to market. In my experience there are mixed feelings about focus groups. Often there is concern about the data being biased by members of the group that dominate the discussion, and many feel that they are similar to brainstorming sessions with people throwing out ideas that they may say they find interesting but if you said I've actually got one in my trunk to sell you right now, no one would open up their wallet.

These concerns have merit. But the basis for them is often more in the organization's ability to gather and act on customer and prospect information rather than some shortcoming in the focus group process. Being able to get a lot of actionable information out of a focus group requires great skill in communicating with a group of people, and understanding group communication dynamics. If you have never run a focus group before, it would be well worth the money to have a professional group run one for you so that you get the most out of a session. Running successful focus groups could be a book of its own, and is beyond our scope here.

But just as an example: One common focus group activity is to throw a topic out and go around the room having members tell their opinions. This can be ineffective, because commonly, one or two focus group members emerge as dominant and many of the group will echo their opinions regardless of their initial impressions. A better way to do this is to throw the concept out to the group and give them 2 minutes to write down their impressions. Then have the members read the items they have on the list. This increases the probability of getting contrary opinions that may have been discarded under the other method.

The bottom line is that regardless of your opinion on focus groups, they are an attempt to gather more information from the front line. It may be more or less successful than other methods of communicating with customers or prospects but it is far better than no communication.

There is a variation of focus groups that I have seen used for prospecting. Running a focus group that gathers feedback from a specific category of executive, which then qualifies them as a prospect, can be exceptionally effective. But you need to be careful here not to make this a gray area that can be interpreted as shady. Part of the effectiveness of these programs is that many executives consider them networking opportunities and expect to possibly learn something about future products and services. The fact that they may also be compensated for taking part in these programs creates a fine line between providing feedback and being bribed to listen to a sales pitch. As with most programs of this type, being completely transparent from first contact will keep you on the straight and narrow. Tell possible participants the focus group is being sponsored by a vendor and that the vendor will receive their contact info, and may even contact them after the focus group has run. As this may be asking more of a focus group member, you may want to highlight how the networking opportunities will be better than the average focus group, as this group was selected to discuss specific topics and will be a better peer group than the average panel. If done correctly, you are sending the message that gathering the right information to make your customers successful is the most important thing you do, and that usually resonates well with prospective customers.

Maintaining Regular Communication

The best way to keep your current customers is to have regular communication scheduled with them as part of the customer life cycle. At the very least, having a monthly email to customers will keep a bare minimum of dialog open and allow you to test topics for interest, let you remain top of mind so references and champions consider you when opportunities arise, and, by capturing click and open data, give you at least some idea as to the activity level of the customer.

The most significant growth in this area has been the explosion of social media sites such as Facebook and Twitter, which are just an extension of the ability of the customer to put their voice out on the web and has continued to grow since the turn of the century. By the late 1990s technically savvy customers could set up websites for their rants. But today, anyone with knowledge of Facebook or Yelp can vent to the world.

In communicating via social media channels, the biggest wave of change over the next 10 years will be in integrating the intelligence that comes from these tools into CRM systems. Many organizations have social media sites as part of their marketing function, and this works well when only early adopters are using those tools. But as the full customer base begins to use these tools, the ability for a small group of marketing social media people to handle the volume of incoming traffic will not scale, or if it does, will create a redundant system as the volume to call center traffic drops off.

The most important point is that in determining how to integrate these social media channels into the existing customer life cycle, you have an opportunity to re-engineer (I know, I haven't used that one much since the early 1990s either, but it actually does apply here) how interactions with customers are handled. The true value of social media advocates in an organization is not their ability to adopt the latest tool that arrives and is used by less than 20 percent of the customer base. Nor is the value for the social media advocate (worse yet from the organization's point of view), to draft upon the strength of the corporate brand to build his or her own social media following. The value is their ability to adapt the information gleaned from prospects and customers via social media and get this information channeled to the parties that can take action with the prospect or customer to resolve problems, generate more business and delight the customer.

From a personal, selfish point of view, this is something you can take advantage of as a customer right now. I have had situations in which I have had problems with a vendor and not been able to resolve them through the normal channel and resorted to asking for assistance via social media. More than once it has made the lack of procedure and integration obvious. Initially, I have had a customer service rep ignore me or drag their feet but after posting to a social media channel I have received help requests from three or four people in various marketing or social media functions, one or more senior managers, and usually a note of apology from the negligent service rep or one of their bosses. A more efficient approach is to determine how information gathered from social media would be directed through additional channels. This is also your opportunity to examine if you have enough resources available to handle the current volume of communication from your customers and prospects. Once you reach a specific level of volume from any one channel the most important step is to get this data into the CRM system and educate anyone that has contact with prospects or customers on the appropriate use of the channel.

Closing the Loop

From the 50,000-foot view there are two areas where customer feedback can improve your business. One is to improve your ability to communicate about your product or service. Understanding what your customers think about what you do allows you to tailor your message to future prospects, and better yet, have your customers validate your work to these prospects. The other area is in improving the product itself—feedback that improves your product marketing.

From the communications side, validation of your work from your customers means that your business model has been verified. You may have to do some work on pricing and operations to stay profitable, but if you are doing things right, as long as you have customers you should be able to find a way to keep the doors open. A good marketing organization will gather this information and use it to generate the annual marketing plan and synthesize this information into a format that sales can either use or benefit from. If you are interested in more discussion specifically on this topic, John Jantsch's *The Referral Engine* is a good book to read.

On the product marketing front, the product owner should be taking responsibility for gathering this information and putting it toward the next version of the product. Although many product marketing people will make excuses along the lines of the customer not understanding possible options, and therefore not being able to provide input, this example is instructive. Lore has it that if Henry Ford asked what his customers wanted, they would not have said the automobile, but instead asked for a faster horse. This is usually a smoke screen and even companies as notorious on this front as Apple take user feedback into account. One point of clarification here—many organizations do not look for feedback during the "Blue Sky" brainstorming of products, but virtually every company that creates quality products develops prototypes for testing and field use prior to going to market.

As a baseline, gathering information about customer experience using the product or service is used to verify the customer life cycle. Putting together a group of customers and having them use a product, possibly even recording them as they go through the process, and asking them to do specific tasks, will quickly bring to light any shortcomings with the product. It's quite common for the group that engineered a product to take for granted a large number of conventions and usages that a new customer unfamiliar with the product (or maybe even the industry as a whole) will have no knowledge of. This is evident from organizations that make things like the now classic VCRs that never have their clocks programmed, all the way up to companies that go the extra mile putting thought into everything from how the box containing the product works and making it easy for customers to get self-service help when dealing with a problem.

Action Items and Summary of Key 4

Big Ideas:

1. Raise Champions – keeping your customers successful is the key to profitability in the long run
2. Maintain regular communication – your content generation strategy needs to keep your customers, your most effective lead generators, in the know.
3. Sharpen your saw – at least once a year go back to your plan and see what needs to be improved.

Leveraging Technology:

1. Start user groups first as virtual events – virtual cuts out the majority of expenses and allows you to get the value of a user group even if you don't have enough momentum to gather five customers in one geographic area.
2. Always survey – take advantage of surveys in regular communications, polling at events and using other tools to progressively learn more about your customers.
3. Positive feedback from your customers validates your business model; track and amplify the great things that your customers have to say about you.

Applying to your CRM System:

1. Gather enough information about customers to be able to report on Champions, References, Customers and Possible Liabilities.
2. Measure the end of the customer lifecycle. Understand why customers become ex-customers and see if you can extend the lifecycle and/or adjust the product.
3. Extend CRM beyond just the first sale to include milestones for existing customers. The ultimate goal is to know the lifetime value of a customer.

In Closing

Sharpening the Saw

As a business matures, the goal is that the customer life cycle eventually solidifies, the business model is verified and becomes financially sustainable. If you are fortunate enough to reach this point, you follow the old adage that success is not a destination, but a voyage, and now is the time to optimize the business process. This is actually a pitfall for many organizations. As the fear of making payroll fades away, bureaucracy can creep in, as work gets more comfortable. This could be judged as good or evil depending upon your opinion, but the fact is that it's not a problem unless the market changes or a competitor steps up to take territory that was formerly yours. It will come down to what kind of culture senior management wants to create, and the willingness of the rest of the organization to follow.

In following the "voyage" frame of mind, you will increase your odds of defending against the competition, and reduce the probability of being swept away in a market sea change. By continually improving the systems that support the customer life cycle your business can continue to grow and adapt to the market.

In this optimization stage you can look for opportunities to "sharpen the saw." This concept is one of Stephen Covey's *7 Habits of Highly Effective People* and is focused on process improvement. Instead of getting an 11th worker and an 11th saw, you may find that by taking 10 minutes a day to sharpen the 10 saws you have, your 10 workers may be able to do the work of 12 the way you did business before you improved your tools.

The Duty of Leadership

As the leader of a successful organization (and this is not limited to top level managers), it's your duty to **look beyond the current quarter**. Although this advice tends to fall into the "eat less and exercise more" category, it's easy to come up with examples of short sighted quarterly focus every time you open the Wall Street Journal.

Free the organization from the **tyranny of the urgent**. Many organizations tend to focus on urgent problems, but the bigger question is if they are important problems. Most of the time they are not. But urgent small problems (such as managing inbound email) feel like work and deliver a feeling of accomplishment. Taking time out to grapple with more important long-term improvement is the only way to see productivity gains. Getting an inbox to zero does nothing for the bottom line.

As your products change and improve, so will the direction and contact points on the customer life cycle. **Reviewing the customer life cycle on a regular basis** will allow you to respond to these changes and keep operations efficient and effective. This includes confirming that there is constant communication with prospects and customers. Reviewing communications will ensure that outdated or irrelevant messages are removed and everything remains on message.

Confirm that the CRM infrastructure is capturing relevant data and that data is being evaluated and acted upon. Irrelevant fields should be considered clutter and removed from interfaces: as new data points are identified they should be added and tracked (if they correspond to an action point on the customer life cycle). Any time a data point is added it should also include a statement of who is responsible for the data in that field and what type of action is required based on the values in the field. This will ensure that no customer will be left behind or ignored.

Reviewing profitability from the product marketing point is the best place to begin the auditing process, and can have a huge impact on the long-term success of your company. Determining which products are the most profitable will help you protect your cash cows and let you evaluate if new offerings are as successful as you originally thought they would be in the marketplace. Mergers and acquisitions also fall into this category as an organization grows. This is where the high stakes poker happens with most companies betting their future. Fortunes and markets are won and lost here.

This same level of analysis can then be done in the market for each product. Examine the makeup of the customer base to determine which customers are most profitable, and which are better off not being customers. This goes right to the core of having a profitable product and will also affect your product strategy by helping you determine which markets to focus upon.

As your organization grows these review cycles can be coordinated with your **Annual Plan.** As you get into the realm of huge corporations, the annual report becomes a part of the planning cycle so synchronizing this with your review can make these reports more than just a bunch of graphs to satisfy reporting requirements.

Look to the horizon to see what's next. If you've reached the point where you've got a strong annual cycle going, you can start to look for larger themes over the next five years and start to consider other markets, mergers and acquisitions, or creating subsidiaries to explore radical new products (to avoid the *Innovator's Dilemma*).

As you chart a course, remember to **communicate the "why" of your organization** on a regular basis to everyone involved. If everyone has an understanding of what the company is trying to do, your business model will scale effectively and your prospects will find it easy to determine if there is a fit for your product or solution. Leaders in the organization are the ones who can effectively communicate the reason you band together as a company. Best of luck to you on your voyage, and if you have any questions or interesting stories, be sure to tell me about them.

John
john@themshow.com

p.s. To continue the voyage, check out the latest at
www.B2BMarketingConfessions.com